Anyone in ministry leadership knows ~~that~~ training and giftedness—vital as they a~~re~~ ~~are not enough to spare~~ leaders from problems and challenges they didn't see coming or those dark nights of the soul they must keep to themselves. *Lifelong Leadership* is a godsend. You hold in your hands a step-by-step, practical guide to create and launch a Mentoring Community—a time-tested practice that has been used globally to end leadership isolation and that benefits emerging leaders with the wisdom and support they long for and need.

> **CAROLYN CUSTIS JAMES,** author of *Half the Church: Recapturing God's Global Vision for Women* and *Malestrom: Manhood Swept into the Currents of a Changing World*

Leighton Ford is widely regarded as the greatest mentoring leader of his generation. He and his ministry partners MaryKate Morse and Anne Grizzle have inspired me and countless emerging leaders to lead more like and more to Jesus. This powerfully insightful and immensely practical book will empower you to help a new generation discover their God-given beauty and power and make their unique contribution to the world.

> **KEN SHIGEMATSU,** pastor of Tenth Church, Vancouver, BC; author of *Survival Guide for the Soul*

YES. Mentoring, in community, is essential—not optional—for every frontline ministry leader. In *Lifelong Leadership*, MaryKate Morse casts a vision for the purpose, power, and practical shape of life-changing, sometimes even life-saving, Mentoring Communities. Stop going it alone and start growing in a group.

> **ANGIE WARD, PhD,** leadership author and teacher

Woven Together
through
MENTORING
COMMUNITIES

Lifelong Leadership

MaryKate Morse

AFTERWORD BY LEIGHTON FORD

NavPress

A NavPress resource published in alliance
with Tyndale House Publishers

NavPress is the publishing ministry of The Navigators, an international Christian organization and leader in personal spiritual development. NavPress is committed to helping people grow spiritually and enjoy lives of meaning and hope through personal and group resources that are biblically rooted, culturally relevant, and highly practical.

For more information, visit NavPress.com.

Lifelong Leadership: Woven Together Through Mentoring Communities

Copyright © 2020 by MaryKate Morse. All rights reserved.

A NavPress resource published in alliance with Tyndale House Publishers, Inc.

NAVPRESS and the NavPress logo are registered trademarks of NavPress, The Navigators, Colorado Springs, CO. *TYNDALE* is a registered trademark of Tyndale House Publishers. Absence of ® in connection with marks of NavPress or other parties does not indicate an absence of registration of those marks.

The Team:
Don Pape, Publisher
David Zimmerman, Acquisitions Editor
Elizabeth Schroll, Copy Editor
Eva Winters, Designer

This work is published in association with Firefly Life Literary, 730 North Maple Street, Saugatuck, Michigan, 49453.

Cover photograph of tapestry copyright © Stanislaw Mikulski/Adobe Stock. All rights reserved.

Author photo taken by George Fox University, copyright © 2018. All rights reserved.

Unless otherwise indicated, all Scripture quotations are taken from the New Revised Standard Version Bible, copyright © 1989, Division of Christian Education of the National Council of the Churches of Christ in the United States of America. Used by permission. All rights reserved. Scripture quotations marked EHV are from the Holy Bible, Evangelical Heritage Version® (EHV®) © 2019 Wartburg Project, Inc. All rights reserved. Used by permission. Scripture quotations marked ESV are from the ESV® Bible (The Holy Bible, English Standard Version®), copyright © 2001 by Crossway, a publishing ministry of Good News Publishers. Used by permission. All rights reserved. Scripture quotations marked MSG are taken from *THE MESSAGE*, copyright © 1993, 2002, 2018 by Eugene H. Peterson. Used by permission of NavPress. All rights reserved. Represented by Tyndale House Publishers. Scripture quotations marked NASB are taken from the New American Standard Bible,® copyright © 1960, 1962, 1963, 1968, 1971, 1972, 1973, 1975, 1977, 1995 by The Lockman Foundation. Used by permission. Scripture quotations marked NIV are taken from the Holy Bible, New International Version,® NIV.® Copyright © 1973, 1978, 1984, 2011 by Biblica, Inc.® Used by permission. All rights reserved worldwide. Scripture quotations marked NLT are taken from the *Holy Bible*, New Living Translation, copyright © 1996, 2004, 2015 by Tyndale House Foundation. Used by permission of Tyndale House Publishers, Carol Stream, Illinois 60188. All rights reserved.

Some of the anecdotal illustrations in this book are true to life and are included with the permission of the persons involved. All other illustrations are composites of real situations, and any resemblance to people living or dead is purely coincidental.

Portions of this book have been quoted from Leighton Ford, *Building & Sustaining a Mentoring Community*, © 2011 by Leighton Ford Ministries. Used by permission. All rights reserved.

For information about special discounts for bulk purchases, please contact Tyndale House Publishers at csresponse@tyndale.com, or call 1-800-323-9400.

ISBN 978-1-64158-017-5

Printed in the United States of America

26	25	24	23	22	21	20
7	6	5	4	3	2	1

Dedicated to
mentors all over the world who love and lift up
the next generation of leaders

Contents

(Unless otherwise indicated, chapters are written by MaryKate Morse.)

Introduction

The Story of Mentoring Communities

Deep and wide
Deep and wide
There's a fountain flowing
Deep and wide

CHILDREN'S SONG BY SIDNEY E. COX

Christian leaders need safe places, safe times, and safe people to help them grow spiritually and be fruitful over the long run.

FROM DECEMBER 3–8, 2016, a group of us gathered at the Bellfry (a retreat home) to focus on writing this book. Each morning we met for prayer. On Sunday morning, the second Sunday of Advent, we read the lectionary reading for that day, Luke 3:1-6, which tells of John the Baptist's mission to proclaim repentance and prepare the way of the Lord. We all believed we were called to prepare the way of Christ so that many might come to know his love and grace. We were all on differing journeys, like John the Baptist, to be faithful. Our lead mentor, Leighton Ford, noted those things about us and then reflected on the serendipitous way the six of us were brought together throughout the years of Leighton's ministry.

Two of us—Anne Grizzle and MaryKate Morse—had separately approached Leighton after he spoke at a conference (one on the East Coast and one on the West Coast) to ask a follow-up question. From those simple questions came years of deep friendship.

Two of us—Raphaël Anzenberger and Chris Woodhull—were students in different programs from different places. Each applied for a scholarship and a leadership program created by Leighton. Both were instrumental in the thinking and experiences found in this book.

One of us—Nick Valadez—applied to be Leighton's assistant.

At a transition point in Leighton's life, he gathered us and several others together to discern his and Jeanie's next step in life. He had been an evangelist with the Billy Graham crusades. He had developed a training and mentoring program, Arrow, for gifted young leaders going into ministry and evangelism. Now he believed God was preparing him for something more focused.

With much prayer and conversation, we discerned the next step: training people to create Mentoring Communities that support developing leaders. We believed that this was the missing component from most leadership-training programs. We also believed the pressing need for leaders was a spiritually mature mentor and companions for the long, difficult haul of ministry. Leaders everywhere felt alone.

On March 29, 2006, in Rock Hill, South Carolina, five of us and Leighton made a commitment together to become the Mentoring Community team. We would figure out how to train other possible mentors to create Mentoring Communities in their areas of ministry. Our calling was

> to advocate and practice the art of Christ-centered spiritual
> mentoring from generation to generation so as to enhance the
> spiritual, emotional, and relational health of kingdom-seeking
> leaders who have a passion to lead for Jesus, like Jesus, and to
> Jesus and, through his Spirit, to be a part of God's transforming
> presence in their communities around the world.

We began by offering five-day gatherings of invited possible mentors to experience a Mentoring Community, so that they might return to their contexts and create one themselves. We did this for ten years, attracting leaders from all over the world. The Mentoring Community format resonated deeply with people.

None of us knew then how God would knit our hearts together in friendship and in mission. We all felt clear that we were Way-Makers as John the Baptist said in Luke 3:4: "Make ready the way of the Lord" (NASB). We were to prepare the way of the Lord through creating Mentoring Communities for evangelists and Christian influencers and through training other mentors to do the same. We felt the urgency to support the lonely, difficult work of those who are doing pioneer mission work as church planters, evangelists, social-justice workers, artists, influencers using social media, et cetera. We became to each other a Mentoring Community. We each had a vision for this project, and each was involved in the creation of this book. I, MaryKate Morse, had the call to take the role of editor and primary author.

Our Vision and Mission

Ministry leaders need safe times, safe places, and safe people to keep going for the long run.

Following the leadership and model of Leighton Ford, we have found that Mentoring Communities provide a significant leadership resource for the health and well-being of developing and even established leaders. Through Mentoring Communities, leaders are exposed to a transforming friendship with God and others. This book casts a dynamic vision for this type of leadership formation and development and clearly outlines the architecture required to create effective Mentoring Communities.

A Mentoring Community is a yearly, three-to-five-day gathering of a mature leader mentor and five to ten younger leader participants who step away from work and daily life and come together to rest, listen, and pray for each other.

The community agrees to meet yearly at dedicated times and in retreat-like places to be a safe people together where prayer and safe conversations are the norm. After the retreat, a Mentoring Community stays connected (usually through social media—discussed in chapter 12) for ongoing support, wisdom, discernment, and prayer. The Mentoring Community members become companions for the difficult and challenging work of ministry.

Since 2008, we have been training experienced, mature leaders in the art of developing Mentoring Communities for emerging leaders, and we have focused particularly on those who have a call to evangelism and frontline ministries. These mature leaders are passionate about creating support systems for the next generation of Christian leaders, who often experience great pressure and frenzied busyness and who feel isolated and alone.

We have trained several hundred evangelists and Christian influencers from more than twenty countries to experience the power of Mentoring Communities. Through the Global Evangelists Forum, the Lausanne Movement, and other trusted partners, we have trained outside the United States with local partners in India, Singapore, Burkina Faso, Kenya, Ghana, France, Mexico, Australia, Canada, and many other places around the world.

Dr. Ford leads two Mentoring Communities, one in its thirtieth year and another in its eighteenth year. Participants include now world-renowned leaders who have had a great impact on the evangelical movement and Christian discipleship. Leighton's model is the vision for the Mentoring Community components described in this book.

Mentoring Communities have proven profoundly formational for leaders. Following Dr. Ford's example, other mentor leaders created their own groups in the United States and internationally, and these new groups help participants experience God in their ministry lives for the long haul. My group has met for eleven years.

It is clear to us that God is in this because of the stories we continue to hear from leaders around the world. This work came to us by the guidance of the Holy Spirit. We saw the fruit of it, and we struggled to understand its scope and content. We realized then that we were doing our small part to prepare God's way for this day and time all over the world by coming alongside others immersed in God's Kingdom work. Today, we are continually blessed by the stories of leaders everywhere who are nourished and helped by these experiences.

> *Not only have I been pastored but also pruned; moulded and motivated; I have been so inspired that I started my own mentoring group with sixteen evangelists who have met annually for three days for twenty years. And several of those I mentor have also birthed their own groups, so the tapestry of mentoring continues.*
>
> REV. CANON J. JOHN (ENGLAND)

In African society, the elders mentor everyone. There is a general understanding of values in the society, and the elders are trusted to pass these values on. We've lost the commonality of values and the role of elders. This is a very great loss. When I came here [to the Mentoring Community training in Karen, Kenya], I put a date on my paper to put all my thoughts in the notebook. Today, after three days, I have nothing [written] down, so it looks like nothing has happened. But what I have learned these days are notes written on my heart. It isn't written on a page. I'm ambushed by a new approach, and I am very grateful.

BISHOP JOHN, PASTOR AND LEADER (KENYA)

Value of Mentoring Communities

Mentoring Communities provide places for developing leaders to safely share what is on their hearts and what is happening in their lives. In these groups, leaders experience support and prayer without fear of judgment or loss of face. In a community of love that continues from one year to the next, these leaders find accountability for holy living and integration of their inner and outer worlds while engaging in God's mission.

Our experience has demonstrated that most Christian leaders worldwide do not listen for the Spirit or create reflective times and places for fellowship and prayer with no other agenda. Neither do they know how to express God's love to each other by giving encouragement and support in safe environments. Every younger and/or inexperienced leader we meet is hungry for a mentor, yet unfortunately, most experienced leaders are not committed to a plan to develop the next generation of Christian leaders or don't know how to do that well.

- *The primary need for younger leaders is companionship and safe support for their spiritual and ministry journeys.* Many developing leaders do not have church communities that "get" them and that know how to support them in their ministry calling.

- *The primary need for mature leaders is a highly effective, low-lift way to mentor several younger leaders at one time.* Mentoring assures that the church's ministry or the organization's mission continues by preparing the next generation of leaders.

The Mentoring Communities described in this book meet these two presenting needs exceptionally well.

Leaders from ages twenty-five to forty-five (and sometimes older) often feel alone. They have been in ministry for five years or longer. Idealism has passed. They have few or no safe places or safe people with whom to process their spiritual and life-stage journeys. They are hungry for conversations with mature leaders. They long for experienced leaders to listen to them and pray for them. They lack a safe community of peers who know their stories and are cheering for their

> *We heat our house with the same wood. . . .*
> *When you bring leaders together in a group,*
> *you have an impact that multiplies it.*
>
> BARRY (CANADA)

spiritual success. These lacks often result in burnout and emotional fatigue, cynicism, spiritual dryness, or unfortunately, loss of integrity and a shift to self-promotional leadership habits.

At the beginning of their ministry journeys, younger leaders attend and are active in the local church and yet often feel constrained by older churchgoers who don't quite understand them and policies that are bureaucratic and risk averse. They are hungry for a deeper life with Christ. Because of this book's solid biblical foundation and exegesis and clearly written, experience-based guidance, younger leaders will benefit from reading and implementing the wisdom and step-by-step process detailed in it. Older leaders with a heart to lift up the next generation of leaders will recognize an easy and effective way to invest in other leaders' lives in the pages that follow.

> Mentoring one-on-one is effective, but I wanted to multiply evangelists. Mentoring Communities are an effective, sustainable way to do just that. I have been training young evangelists of every stripe and placing them in Mentoring Communities for over ten years. We began with a handful of evangelists; we now have over a hundred and are mentoring even more.
>
> RAPHAËL, EVANGELIST (FRANCE)

Mentoring Communities began as a global effort with Leighton Ford's first group of young leaders from all over the world: Germany, Australia, Singapore, England, and the US. The interest in Mentoring Community training has expanded to all continents except Antarctica. This widespread demand makes it impossible for the training team to respond to all the requests. Therefore, this book serves as a comprehensive, step-by-step, practical guide for experienced leaders in any country to learn how to create and launch a Mentoring Community, including direction regarding its purpose, nature, and components.

Mature Christian leaders will be able to gather others and lead the group through the experiences outlined here. This book also works for peers who have no access to a mentor but want to create a peer Mentoring Community. The outcome will be highly functional Mentoring Communities for emerging leaders throughout the world by the formation of safe times, safe places, and safe people. The book describes what these groups are, why they are important, and how they work.

There are many books on mentoring but none on how to create a Mentoring Community. This book is unique because it

- uses a prayer-and-listening formational model for mentoring, where once a year, every year, the group commits to several days together in a retreat setting;

- uses a lead mentor and peer mentors who commit to meet in community for the long haul;

- works as a mentoring model for men and women leaders in mixed, gender-focused, or affinity groups;

- works cross-culturally and globally in diverse settings from privileged to less privileged environments;

- works for seminary- or Bible school–educated leaders or for leaders with little or no education;

- is especially helpful and meaningful for those in frontline ministries, such as evangelists, church planters, Christian artists, entrepreneurs, and reformers; and

- offers replicable, uncomplicated guidance for creating Mentoring Communities.

This book serves as a guide. It will continue to grow through the experiences of those who take it to heart. We would very much like to hear from you, should you have insights and experiences to add to this resource. We've included as many personal stories as possible. They either were submitted by the individuals named with the express purpose of inclusion in this book or are composites with fictional names that represent the types of things we've seen and heard in Mentoring Communities. None of the stories break confidentiality agreements.

May the Lord bless and keep you as you "prepare the way of the LORD" in whatever manner God has called you (Isaiah 40:3).

PART ONE

The Need for Leaders & the Needs of Leadership

1

The Urgent Need
of Emerging Leaders

*When there is no distinction in conduct between Christians and
non-Christians—for example in the practice of corruption and
greed, or sexual promiscuity, or rate of divorce, or relapse to pre-
Christian religious practice, or attitudes towards people of other
races, or consumerist lifestyles, or social prejudice—then the world is
right to wonder if our Christianity makes any difference at all.*

CAPE TOWN COMMITMENT, 2010

WHEN I BECAME A CHRISTIAN at the age of eighteen, it was a liberating day. I felt happy and free. Before my step of faith, I had had many dark and harmful experiences. I was broken, sinful, and far from God. I couldn't find anything to fill the hole in me—until I accepted Christ. I had tried the world, relationships, other faiths, and other ideologies. Finally, while in college, I accepted a simple invitation to trust Jesus, and I haven't turned back.

I was eager for the journey, and since I was away at college, I wasn't always sure what to do next or who might help me. Unfortunately, I soon realized I was on my own. I often wondered how different my journey might have been if I had had someone to mentor me in those early years. I felt very much alone, though I did join a Christian student group and got very involved in its activities, local and statewide. I was engaged and busy, but I was not discipled.

I felt as if I were stumbling along. I had many questions, but mostly I remember wishing I had someone who would guide me. For me, that didn't happen until I was in my late thirties and early forties, as a married adult with children—which is a long time to wait for mentoring companionship. Because of that experience, I have determined to be a mentor to younger leaders and even older ones who are just beginning to find their way.

The first thing that happened to me after my conversion was a clear memory of God's call on my life when I was a girl of ten. My parents had taken me to a church to honor a missionary who was retiring after twenty-five years as a single woman on a mission in the Truk Islands.[1] She was small in stature, with white hair pulled back in a bun. I don't even remember her name. She told story after story of loving and serving the islanders, and then we had cake. As I listened to her sharing about her ministry, the Lord spoke to me and said, "You will serve me like this one day." This was the first time I heard God. When I accepted Christ into my life at eighteen, the call returned, real and urgent. I have committed myself to the church and to God's mission in the world ever since.

Without mentoring, I was an earnest but ineffective evangelist. I locked my sister in the bathroom so I could tell her about Jesus, and she yelled at me to let her out. I upset my grandmother by standing in front of the television while she was watching her favorite show, trying to tell her that she needed Jesus. She got so frustrated that she threw her slipper at me. I'm sure that those without guides and mentors are still watched over by God, but I wonder how differently my life might have gone if someone had taken an interest in me and my call. When I responded to Jesus' invitation in college, I remembered my call, though my effectiveness as an evangelist and Christian leader was sorely lacking for many years.

Without mentoring, I stumbled, trying to figure out how to lead well. I didn't know to whom I could turn when I had troubling questions about faith or when I had difficulties with some people. Also, after my conversion, I was surprised at the poor quality of Christian witness that I experienced in some older, more seasoned leaders. In my naiveté, I believed that the longer you walked with Jesus, the more saintly you became.

I expected pastors and Christian influencers with years of study, prayer, and close fellowship with Jesus to be holy, kind, generous, and capable. It shook me to my core to have a youth pastor try to assault me and a married church leader show inappropriate affection to me. It rocked me that the adult leader in the Baptist Student Union was an angry, withdrawn woman.

I am no longer naive about such things, but I continue to be troubled by the shallow character and tepid commitment of some Christian leaders, who profess righteousness but live otherwise. As I mature as a spiritual leader, I am also aware of my own weaknesses and struggles. I am now one of those older leaders who don't always lead or serve well. Serving for Christ is a lifelong battle of interior forces and outside challenges. It is not uncommon to read of well-known Christian leaders who fail.

I remember when Ted Haggard, the leader of the National Association of Evangelicals (2003–2006) in North America and the pastor of a megachurch called New Life Church in Colorado Springs, Colorado, USA, fell. He had all the resources at his disposal to prevent his life from imploding. He was happily married with children. He had prestige and access to all the major political and cultural leaders of that day. He had money to pay for counseling and spiritual direction. Surely, he knew seasoned, saintly leaders to whom he could turn for help. Even if he simply confided in a few trusted friends and asked for prayer and help, his life story might have turned out differently.

Instead, in November 2006, a male prostitute, Mike Jones, let the

3

world know that Ted Haggard had paid him for sex over a three-year period and for the drug crystal meth.[2] Haggard denies some of the details but none of the substance.

How did this happen? What damage do things like this do to the witness of the church? Where were Ted's accountability persons? How had his elders failed him? What might have happened differently if he had people in his life with whom he could confess and get help early while on this journey to ruin? The forces of our own Western culture press us into its mold wherever we live. In the West, our independent mind-set and lone-ranger lifestyles make it easy to isolate our personal lives from our public lives. We don't need anyone.

The commercialized tendency in the church to elevate a charismatic male to the top to attract more people is a recipe for moral failure or character flaw. The world's need to have messiah figures gets translated in the church to promoting a single male authoritarian leader at the top. This need elevates and then isolates leaders, not allowing them to publicly falter or doubt. If a leader confesses doubts or struggles, elders often react rather than come alongside and aid the leader.

In a community of brothers and sisters, there is strength. We were designed to need one another, so it is no wonder that we falter when we are expected to stand alone. Ted believes God has forgiven him, and his family has. He is pastoring a small church and trying to make something of his life. Of course God forgives, and a leader can seek God's mercy and grace. But how do you restore the image people had of the Christian faith's effectiveness to change their lives when those they trust fail?

The purpose of this chapter is to make a clear case for the urgent need for today's leaders to have safe times and places to go apart and have safe people with whom they may be honest and transparent about what is going on in their inner world. Being a part of a Mentoring Community might have made a difference in Ted Haggard's life. It certainly would have helped me.

Urgent Need for Evangelists and Christian Leaders

Africa is the world's fastest-growing continent.
Sixty percent of the African population is below
twenty-five years old. Who is Jesus to our generation?
How do we help them stay faithful?

EMMANUEL, PASTOR (RWANDA)

When Jesus ascended into heaven and the Holy Spirit fell on the disciples at Pentecost, the early believers eventually went out like a flood to tell everyone the Good News of Jesus Christ. After the infilling of the Holy Spirit, this Good News poured out from Jerusalem, according to Jesus' words: "You will receive power when the Holy Spirit has come upon you; and you will be my witnesses in Jerusalem, in all Judea and Samaria, and to the ends of the earth" (Acts 1:8). To witness is to bear testimony to what you have heard and seen and know to be true in your own life.

The early church flourished on this compulsion to share the wondrous message of Jesus Christ, who died for us, rose for us, and brings us before the very eyes of God as holy, blameless, and beyond reproach. They flourished not only on the words but also on the wondrous changes Christians brought to the culture. Christians cared for orphans and widows. No one else was doing that. Christians went into prisons and cared for the incarcerated. No one else was doing that. Christians cared for the sick, even during infectious plagues. Everyone else ran away. Christ made a difference in the lives of individuals and in the communities in which they lived.

When persecution began in Jerusalem, believers went everywhere, bearing witness to Jesus Christ and changing their communities. Everyone was an evangelist. Evangelism meant being the Good News all day, every day. Everyone was a bearer of Good News, whatever one's place or work in life. The early church had men and women, old and young, slave and free living and proclaiming the gospel and serving the suffering and outsiders in their communities.

Paul expanded the territory for bringing hope. He felt called to preach to the Gentiles. On the Damascus Road, he who himself was a persecutor met a living Lord who told him to go into the city to receive guidance. When Jesus told Ananias to go and heal the very one bent on destroying persons like himself, Ananias obeyed. Jesus said to him, "Go, for he is an instrument whom I have chosen to bring my name before Gentiles and kings and before the people of Israel" (Acts 9:15).

Paul, the first missionary evangelist and apologist, gave his life to spreading the gospel of Jesus Christ wherever the Spirit led him. He always traveled with others. He listened to the Holy Spirit, and he fearlessly led the early church and proclaimed the Good News. The gospel spread from Jerusalem to the remotest part of the world. We follow the same pattern. This is our urgency, to be people who share the Good News and influence communities with the wisdom, compassion, and justice of God.

This urgency is as strong and important today as it was in the early church. The world needs evangelists and Christian leaders who are at full capacity. The world needs women and men, old and young, rich and poor who give their lives to lead

> *My calling is to mobilize evangelists. They are an endangered species, often without direction and lonely. There are many challenges. They rise up like a rocket and come down like pieces of wood. It is vital for evangelists to mentor and nurture evangelists. Not only evangelists, but how do we mentor politicians to be a continuing witness? How do we mentor judges, policemen, et cetera?*
>
> STEPHEN, AFRICAN ENTERPRISE DIRECTOR (KENYA)

like Jesus, for Jesus, and to Jesus. Our faith is not a private affair. It is not for our own personal benefit. Our faith is for the benefit of all humankind. We are a "kingdom of priests" (Exodus 19:6, NIV). We are lights set on a hill (Matthew 5:14-16). We have work to do. The work of sharing the Good News (the "going") and being the Good News

6

(the "abiding") is what Jesus modeled for us and what the Holy Spirit anoints us to do.

The field is as ready today as it was in the first century. In the world, there are 2.3 billion Christians, and there are 4.7 billion persons who have not met Jesus Christ. Christianity has quadrupled in the last one hundred years, but because of global population growth, Christians still only make up about 32 percent of the world's population.[3]

Wherever you go, whomever you meet, whatever kindness you extend, you bring the living presence of Christ embodied in and through you. There are two messages: a message proclaimed and a message lived. Christ is proclaimed somewhat with words and more so with a life lived in holiness and love. There are people everywhere, people made in the image of God, yearning to meet a loving and present Lord. Some of these people only *you* will meet. Will they experience the nature of Christ through you?

There are also catastrophic needs everywhere that Jesus mandated us to address by loving our neighbors (Matthew 19:19). When God created us, he commanded us to have dominion over all the earth. We are to take care of the earth and the people on it. We are message bearers with the work that we do on behalf of Christ. We need to be at our best to proclaim a gospel of grace and justice. As the early Christians did, our task is to care for the world and its suffering, not build insular churches where we focus on living happy lives.

For example, one-half of the world lives in poverty. Every day, twenty-two thousand children die because of disease, violence, war, and lack of health care. There is work to do to be the Good News to innocents everywhere. There are 72 million primary-school-age children who are not in school. The world needs teachers and tutors and "aunties and uncles" and doctors and nurses to care for these children. These are not just challenges in other countries. These are challenges in Western neighborhoods as well. We are message bearers meant to give prophetic voice and find solutions to the social challenges of our day. These challenges beckon us but also demand of us that we be at our best, like Christ.

The need for evangelists and Christian leaders is no different today than it was at the time of the early church. We need every Christian to have a sense of his or her partnership in the work of God's Kingdom. There is much to be done, and we are given capacity and the Holy Spirit's help to play our part. The need for Christian leaders, however, is primarily the need for *Christlike* evangelists, ministers, and Christian influencers.

Urgent Need for Christlike Evangelists, Ministers, and Christian Influencers

> *There will be no Christlike mission without Christlike leaders.*
> NANA YAW OFFEI, LAUSANNE LEADER (GHANA)

There is much to do in almost every way and for people everywhere, in your neighborhood, town, and country. We all have a part to play in God's Kingdom as long as we have breath. It is not enough to speak truth and to fight for justice. We must also commit to being like Christ. It is not enough to know Christ. We must also be completely submitted to the ongoing work of Christ in us, and this is not easy. We are more easily held captive by the world's picture of success and by the limitations of our own agendas. In Jesus' day, not everyone could "see" him. In John 9:39-41, Jesus tried to explain this to the Pharisees: "I came into this world for judgment so that those who do not see may see, and those who do see may become blind."

Some of the Pharisees near him heard this and said to him, "Surely we are not blind, are we?" Jesus said to them, "If you were blind, you would not have sin. But now that you say, 'We see,' your sin remains."

Some religious people today—Christians—do not "see" Jesus. This can happen to us. Our capacities, callings, and egos can easily supplant Christ's primacy in our lives. We replace a living Lord with our own ideas about faith and ministry. We like our seats at the head of the table. We like our names honored and mentioned. We like people

8

paying attention to our spoken words, written words, and podcasts. This can move the message off Christ and onto us. This temptation is a result of the Fall and thus is woven into the very fabric of our humanity.

Super Chickens

A researcher at Purdue University, William Muir, studies the productivity of chickens.[4] He wants to know how to breed chickens that lay lots of eggs and create environments that foster greater productivty. To research how to make "super chickens," he did an experiment.

Muir put chickens into two groups. One group contained normal, healthy chickens. He left them alone for six generations of a chicken's life. Another, separate group included all the super chickens, those who were proven high-producing egg layers. Muir left them alone for six generations. He provided food, water, and a clean environment but did nothing to influence the chickens' egg laying.

At the end of the experiment, Muir discovered that the group of normal chickens were flourishing: They were laying more eggs per chicken than when the experiment started. In the group of super chickens, only three were left. They had pecked the others to death. The super chickens had laid more eggs through a strategy of suppressing other chickens' productivity,[5] by killing or intimidating them so they were unable to lay eggs.

When we think of leadership, we can fall into the same trap. We believe that if we find the right super chickens, we will have success. We look for the superstars.[6] We give them the best resources and empower them, believing that they will uniquely bring hundreds to Christ or to our churches, or that they will bring in hundreds of dollars for our ministries. The truth is the same in the human world as it is in the chicken world, however: This strategy leads only to dysfunction.

This is the strategy that led to the fall of Bill Hybels, who even wrote a book on character, *Who You Are When No One's Looking*.[7] His public and his private lives were not the same. With Hybels's privileged place of authority and access as the leader of a megachurch, he lost touch with his primary purpose, to love others as Jesus loved.[8]

Privilege means assuming that someone is a super chicken, that someone has a right to their own point of view, their own way of behaving or misbehaving. In our culture—and often, in our churches—we create super chickens because we desperately want success. We think it can come through one superstar leader. This usually doesn't go well. People get hurt, and this is not the way of Jesus.

Jesus did not profit from his position of power as the Son of God. He humbled himself, even to death, to love and serve us (Philippians 2:8). When we sway from the posture of Jesus, we create two problems: (1) fewer Christian leaders and (2) Christian leaders who are less like Christ.

The Christian-leadership crisis is that we are looking for super chickens rather than developing and mentoring the chickens who are producing eggs. This includes all kinds of evangelists and influencers, women as well as men, the poor as well as the wealthy, the ethnically diverse as well as the dominant culture, the uneducated as well as those in academic settings. When we relinquish our need to have "stars" to make us right or successful, we learn to see leaders in all corners.

Sadly, today, few Christian leaders develop other leaders because they are so busy with their own responsibilities. The temptation is to do and do in order to be seen and honored. These leaders might have younger, less experienced leaders in their entourages, but the size of the entourage is sometimes more for show than for raising up the next generation of leaders. Little is done to relationally invest in these younger leaders or provide opportunities for them to learn skills and develop. The younger leaders must either wait until the super chicken dies or go find another place to lead.

During the life of Jesus, the angst of the Pharisees and Sadducees was both theological and personal. The religious leaders believed that Jesus just had it wrong, and he was threatening all the work they had done for their Jewish faith to thrive, even under Roman occupation. We know it was personal when we read such things as

> Every day he was teaching in the temple. The chief priests, the scribes, and the leaders of the people kept looking for a way to kill him; but they did not find anything they could do, for all the people were spellbound by what they heard.
>
> LUKE 19:47-48

These leaders were angry, jealous, and afraid because the people were spellbound by Jesus and followed him in droves. They could threaten to kill Jesus, and eventually, they did so to "protect" their religious life, as if God had no power or was not active. We cannot judge because in our own way, we can become like these religious leaders. When we separate our theology and behavior from a living experience of Christ and a commitment to a lifelong journey of humble submission to Christ's work in us, we can become proud, arrogant, and self-sufficient. We can become super chickens, even if we are in a little henhouse.

Discipleship of the contemporary church is so thin, and burnout and failure rates of Christian leaders so high, that loneliness and demoralization among Christian leaders is considered acceptable. We assume that a particular skill set is super, and then we force our leaders to chase those skills to the exclusion of other, more life-giving skills.

Jesus modeled what it is like to be a Christian influencer or evangelist. We see what Jesus sees. We are about healing, gathering in, helping others, preaching and teaching for life, reforming communities, serving the unserved and the poor, just as Jesus did. But in both our lives and the Bible, Christian leaders often become more consumed with guarding their place than serving the least of these.

A group of researchers at the Massachusetts Institute of Technology replicated the chicken experiment with leaders to see what would happen.[9] They put volunteers in two groups and gave them a hard problem to solve. One group consisted of people with normal intelligence. The other group consisted of people with super intelligence (very impressive IQs).

The outcome was similar to that of the super chicken experiment. The smarter the people in a group, the less able they were to solve the assigned problems because they kept trying to impress each other. The people with average intelligence solved the problems. The researchers found three factors that led to the success of the normal-intelligence group: (1) they cared for each other; (2) they gave equal time to each other, so no one person dominated; and (3) successful groups had more women in them. Even MIT researchers recognized that super chickens do not lead to the best outcomes.

Billy Graham, whom some might consider a super chicken because of his platform and fame, worked tirelessly to support and resource other leaders. He had a vision to unite Christian leaders around the world to learn and contextualize mission and ministry in a rapidly changing world and to encourage and strengthen each other.

Thus began an international effort to work together in the manner of Christ: the Lausanne Movement. The first gathering, in July 1974, had 2,700 participants from 150 countries. John Stott chaired a diverse committee of thinkers who created "The Lausanne Covenant,"[10] which is considered one of the most important documents of the church.[11] It was a covenant they made together with God and with each other.

The third Lausanne Congress met in Cape Town, South Africa, October 16–25, 2010, with four thousand leaders attending from 198 countries. Another document was written: the Cape Town Commitment, which outlines biblical concerns and strategies and gives direction to the concerns of Lausanne for the next ten years. A recognized problem in that document is the tendency of Christian ministries to groom super chickens rather than humble servant leaders. The participants understood that the Good News is embodied in those who live Christ and tell about Christ. Telling is not enough. The Good News is holistic, and these leaders acknowledged that in the Cape Town Commitment:

"The salvation we proclaim should be transforming us in the totality of our personal and social responsibilities. Faith without works is dead."[12]

We know we need Christ-centered leaders and evangelists. Yet the Commitment reads, "Arguably the scale of un-Christlike and worldly leadership in the global Church today is glaring evidence of generations of reductionist evangelism, neglected discipling and shallow growth. The answer to leadership failure is not just more *leadership* training but better *discipleship* training. Leaders must first be disciples of Christ himself."[13] The work of God's Kingdom is not to create little kingdoms, building personal empires, but to usher in God's Kingdom together.

Challenges

Not only is it difficult to be Christlike; Christian leaders face many challenges. Research conducted by LifeWay Research among US pastors in 2015 found

- 84 percent say they're on call 24 hours a day.
- 80 percent expect conflict in their church.
- 54 percent find the role of pastor frequently overwhelming.
- 53 percent are often concerned about their family's financial security.
- 48 percent often feel the demands of ministry are more than they can handle.
- 21 percent say their church has unrealistic expectations of them.[14]

"This is a brutal job," said Scott McConnell, former vice president of LifeWay Research. "The problem isn't that pastors are quitting—the problem is that pastors have a challenging work environment."

Ministry is hard. In a 2017 whole-life assessment of pastors, Barna research found that ministry leaders risk failure in three areas: burnout risk, relationship risk, and spiritual risk.[15] Pastors run out of steam. Pastors' core relationships begin to break down, and the spiritual fuel for their calling, Jesus Christ, becomes an increasingly distant, disconnected figure. Pastors and ministry leaders struggle because of the lack of ongoing, meaningful formation of their own inner journeys, the lack of friends who understand their journey, and the lack of emotional and physical rest. When ministry leaders begin to experience burnout or challenges in their relationship with significant people in their lives or with Christ, they isolate and fall into default behavior patterns to cope.

Ministry is hard because ministers are finite, broken human beings (like everyone who walks this earth) who are subjected to unrealistic personal expectations and audacious mission outcomes set by their congregations and fomented by cultural evangelicalism. In a 2016 study, LifeWay Research found that many pastors leave the pastorate because of a lack of support when facing challenges.[16] Their church leaders, councils, bishops, and superintendents aren't helping them. Christian leaders need safe environments in which they can unpack their inner worlds and their outward realities. They need to be able to pray and play and process together in community. They need to cultivate in community a maturing expression of Christ's character and mission in their lives.

Christian leaders are often tired and alone. They are usually overworked and underpaid, and they wrestle with identity and relationship issues. Some are proud. Some are insecure. Some are depressed and burned out. Some are exhausted. The typical solution of working harder does not solve the problems. Following the next model or program doesn't produce the promised outcomes either. Ministry is an unforgiving calling in its unique level of temptation and suffering.

With the press of responsibility and expectations, the burden can become too much. It's easy to imagine how a person looking for a quick fix might turn to alcohol, drugs (especially prescription drugs), or pornography. These hidden "fixes" create even more entrenched addictive patterns. So what works to support these beloved saints in the field? What avoids the social and spiritual traps of super chickens?

A Solution

We need a way to companion developing leaders for a lifetime journey of keeping their eyes on Jesus; helping them lead like Jesus, to Jesus, and for Jesus. Mentoring Communities create places where a leader's walk, personal and with a mentor and peers, comes together. Mentoring Communities focus on the leader's whole life with the companionship of a mentor and friends.

Personal Walk

As leaders, walking close to Christ in daily life strengthens our character and our witness. The discipleship image used in the Bible is *walking*, following Jesus. When we take a walk, we go from one place to another. We see things. We hear things. We experience things. We have moved. Faith in Christ is a lifelong journey of moving continually closer from the old self to the new, baptized into the living life of Christ.

> If we say that we have fellowship with him while we are walking in darkness, we lie and do not do what is true; but if we walk in the light as he himself is in the light, we have fellowship with one another, and the blood of Jesus his Son cleanses us from all sin.
>
> 1 JOHN 1:6-7

> And this is love, that we walk according to his commandments; this is the commandment just as you have heard it from the beginning—you must walk in it.
>
> 2 JOHN 1:6

The community that has embraced the Cape Town Commitment refers to this lifelong journey as "HIS walk." HIS walk involves paying attention to being persons of humility, integrity, and simplicity.

- Walk in humility, rejecting the idolatry of power . . .
- Walk in integrity, rejecting the idolatry of success . . .
- Walk in simplicity, rejecting the idolatry of greed.[17]

How can we tell if we are people of humility, integrity, and simplicity? When our heart for other people and for God is increasing, we are walking toward the light and with Christ. If we have difficulties with lust, anger, pride, despair, arrogance, or fear, if these feelings overwhelm our choices so we choose an easier path, then we are not walking according to the light. We need a mentor and friends to help us when we are weary.

You can learn a lot about leaders by watching them. Hearing about a leader's accomplishments does not mean he or she is walking faithfully with Christ. Listening to an impressive sermon does not enable you to assess the quality of the speaker's character. But you can learn a lot by watching them. I was a presenter at an event that had three prominent spiritual leaders and about twenty-five international participants who were Christian influencers.

We sat in a circle, and whoever was talking had the full attention of the prominent leaders. Two of the leaders paid attention to each person's comments. During the free time, these leaders chose to go on walks or have conversations with others. They didn't escape to their private rooms. This deeply moved the participants.

One woman said to me, "I don't know who you people are. You have not given us your titles. You sit and eat with us. And you give yourselves freely to help us. Who are you?" She was beginning to see that some of the leaders were well-known people, but they didn't lead with their accomplishments. They led with being present to others.

One of the well-known leaders was very distracted the entire time, however. He sat outside the circle, behind the participants. He was on his phone or computer all the time. He did not look up. During free time, he disappeared to his room. He came late and left early. The only time he was engaged was when he was speaking. Then he was brilliant with his words and insights. In his super-chicken culture, he knew his role was to be brilliant with his words and thoughts. He was not expected to participate with or engage people unless they mattered to the success of his organization. He was conformed to the values and rules of engagement of this world. Worldly leaders know how to be brilliant and full of insights. Jesus expected Christian leaders to be different. Christian leaders are the ones who know they must walk HIS path of humility, integrity, and simplicity.

Community Walk

The personal walk with Christ is embedded in a community walk. Besides a personal walk with Christ, evangelists and Christian influencers must also be in communities where they can be accountable to their peers and a mentor. When they are not, developing leaders might be searching for a super-chicken platform.

Communal accountability is a rare but necessary feature for Christian leaders who desire an authentic walk with Christ. The early church understood the vital importance of discipling believers over a long period of time and of holding leaders accountable. With this book, we are trying to provide a solution to support developing leaders.

In loving communities, leaders can be their true selves in a safe environment. In safe communities, brothers and sisters in service to Christ experience companionship and encouragement. They can bear burdens for one another in prayer and love. A leader's personal walk has integrity when it's done honestly with others who know their story and bear their burdens with them.

Whether we serve in public platforms or humble places, leaders need safe times, safe places, and safe people to have safe conversations, so we do not drift from the light into the dark. When we are on our own and things get tougher and tougher, it is easy to slip into the shadows.

When we are on our own and people are mean or unsupportive, or betray us, or when we are struggling financially and relationally, it is easy to slip into the shadows. We are not meant to be alone. Jesus was not alone, so neither should we expect to do ministry without friendship and supportive mentors. We need to walk our faith journeys in communities.

We need community *so that* our personal walk can flourish. We need not only walk with Jesus; we need not be alone in our walk with Jesus. And for leaders, the call on our discipleship is particularly difficult, so we need a real-life reminder that our ministry and mission are part of something much larger that God is doing in the world. This reminder comes through regularly connecting with other disciples beyond our immediate contexts.

Mentoring Communities are *doing life together* over the long haul with a senior mentor and a community of peers. In the same way that Jesus gathered twelve people around him, a Mentoring Community has an experienced leader and a group of developing leaders. Mentoring is a relationship process by which a spiritual leader walks with and guides a group of developing, less experienced leaders. The following chapter details the components of a Mentoring Community more comprehensively.

Closing Thoughts

When I met Leighton Ford, he was speaking about servant leadership. I had read his book *Transforming Leadership*,[18] and I was writing about Jesus' leadership for my doctoral studies. So after his presentation, I went up to ask him how he thought leaders could be trained to be more like Jesus. I have gone up to other leaders after conferences to ask questions. As a woman, I usually get a short answer, and then the speaker moves on to the next person. This gentle man took time to respond. He then invited me to visit his Arrow Leadership training program in Charlotte, North Carolina, the next time they were in session, so I could see firsthand how he trained leaders.

After arriving in Charlotte, I spent the night, and was told that the next day, someone would pick me up and take me to the training site. What astonished me was that Dr. Ford himself picked me up and drove me there. I was humbled that the second man to Billy Graham on his crusades and the former head of the Lausanne Movement would drive me the two hours to the retreat center. He wanted to get to know me better. He asked me to tell him my story. He asked about my studies. He asked for my thoughts on training Christian leaders. He asked me about my prayer life and where I was growing in my faith. He asked me how he could pray for me.

I asked him about his story, and he shared it with me. Until I met Leighton, I'd never had a senior leader care about who I was or what I thought. I was impressed with his experience, knowledge, and grace-filled wisdom. Upon arrival, we went our separate ways. I showed up for the opening banquet, where students from all over the world—some of the brightest, most entrepreneurial leaders I've ever seen in one place—were seated.

Before the meal started, Leighton said he wanted to introduce the guests. Then he talked a little about me and told the students, "This is someone you must have a conversation with. She is insightful, wise, and spiritually astute. Get your date books out and make sure you have a chance to talk with her." I was surprised and humbled.

After the meal, many students came over with their schedules, asking for a time to meet. Every meal from then on, I ate with someone. I came as an unknown, and then I was known and included. Having an influential person tell others of my value and contribution had a big impact on my leadership development. He shared his space with me and anointed my efforts. From then on, Dr. Ford has been a significant mentor in my life. Because of his support and the communities that he brought me into, I have experienced firsthand the importance and value of Mentoring Communities. Since then, I have not felt alone. I am a better leader, Christ follower, and human being.

2

What Is Spiritual Mentoring?

I have been in seminary. I studied for seven years, and I
never heard about mentoring. When I go back, I will take up
mentoring. When I pastor, I will implement mentoring.

TENGEN, PASTOR (NAGALAND, INDIA)

J. JOHN IS AN INTERNATIONALLY KNOWN evangelist from the United
Kingdom. He has been a member of Leighton Ford's Point Group for
twenty-nine years as of the writing of this book. He wrote this about
mentoring:

> I'm a great fan of mentoring. Mentoring goes against the spirit
> of our age. It's personal when everything seems impersonal:
> Mentoring reaches the "me-I-really-am" rather than the "me-
> someone-thinks-I-am." It is flexible: Where I might be expected
> to fit into a framework, mentoring interacts with me, responding
> to my hopes and fears with the encouragement or challenge that's
> needed. It's authentic when so much is artificial: With mentoring,
> I can talk honestly about what troubles me and get honest
> responses. Mentoring draws on hard-won experience rather than

theoretical expectations: There's a reality and practical wisdom
to mentoring that I don't find elsewhere. Ultimately, mentoring
engages and challenges me in a way that nothing else does. Yes, we
have the mentor in the Holy Spirit—God alongside us—but at its
best, mentoring is an extraordinary channel for the Holy Spirit to
work through.[1]

Mentoring is a relationship process by which a mature spiritual
leader walks with and guides a developing, less experienced spiritual
leader. Spiritual Mentoring is helping people pay attention to what God
is doing in their lives and respond in faith. There is no agenda. The
mentor is not trying to create a clone of himself or herself or a worker
bee to do the spiritual mentor's bidding.

As Raphaël Anzenberger, evangelist in France, has commented,
"Mentoring is a means of multiplying."[2] We can multiply evangelists,
pastors, Christian leaders, social-justice advocates, et cetera through
mentoring because that is what Jesus did. This is what has happened
in my own life, and this is what we can do for others. Without the
mentoring of Dr. Ford, I would not be where I am today and I would
not be multiplying leaders through mentoring. Mentoring makes a
difference.

Mentoring is an ancient practice found in the Bible and in many
cultures around the world. In many cultures, a boy or girl would become
a man or woman by learning certain skills and apprenticing to a master
in those skills. Throughout the Bible, we see clear examples of mentors
developing leaders. For instance, Joshua was mentored by Moses, Elisha
was mentored by Elijah, and Ruth was mentored by Naomi.

The word *mentor* is not found in the Bible, but it does include many
words associated with mentoring, such as *disciple*, *imitator*, and *teacher*.
The key word is the Greek word *mathétés*, which means "disciple" and
is found 264 times throughout all four of the Gospels and Acts. The
word is clearly associated with the work of Christ and the early church.

When we think of discipleship, most of us imagine our individual selves learning how to follow Jesus. But from the beginning of his ministry, Jesus gathered disciples around him and developed them. We can learn a lot by examining John 1:35-37: "The next day John again was standing with two of his disciples, and as he watched Jesus walk by, he exclaimed, 'Look, here is the Lamb of God!' The two disciples heard him say this, and they followed Jesus."

John the Baptist, who had a group of his own disciples, wanted the best for them, so he sent his best to Jesus. He pointed them to Christ, not to himself or to following in his footsteps in his own ministry. John the Baptist knew his calling was to clear the way to Jesus (Matthew 3:11). We share his calling. We point to Jesus—not to ourselves, our churches, our denominations, our agendas, or our missions. Christ is all. When we mentor, we gather younger leaders, not to follow us but to send them to Jesus.

When these eager disciples came to Jesus, he asked them, "What are you looking for?" (John 1:38). Jesus asked them what they wanted. He accepted their curiosity as the beginning of their journey. He did not give them his agenda. He had them come with him to observe and learn. The disciples replied by asking Jesus their own question: "Where are you staying?" They didn't know what they wanted. Their identity and calling were still developing, but they did want to hang out with Jesus and learn from him.

Jesus responded, "Come and see" (John 1:39). Jesus invited them into his life, and they remembered the exact time they began following him. He did not invite them into his ideas or his platform; they joined him in life. Jesus mentored them.

Jesus mentored the Twelve. He had a small group of his disciples that he loved deeply, and he invested his life in mentoring them. He did not run around being the primary speaker at conferences or teaching in rabbinical schools or writing his thoughts. He lived his life as the Spiritual Mentor of the Twelve. He loved them to the end. He modeled for them what it means to fully follow God, through success and through persecution. He trained them. He rebuked them when necessary. He sent them out, and he debriefed with them. He prayed for them and with them. He withheld nothing from them.

We often think of mentoring as a one-on-one process, but in the New Testament, it usually happened in a group. The term *mathétés* appears 239 times in the plural in the Gospels and Acts and only 25 times in the singular form.[3] Paul mentored spiritual leaders in a group context on his missionary journeys: John Mark, Titus, Timothy, Barnabas, Silas, Judas, and Luke accompanied him as disciples and coworkers. Jesus and Paul mentored in groups in the context of their goal to establish the church, a body of believers living together in faith, hope, and love.

Elements of Spiritual Mentoring

The purpose of Spiritual Mentoring is to glorify God by being the church and growing the church. Spiritual mentors come alongside mentees to help them be more like Jesus and to lead others to Jesus. It's not about the mentee simply fulfilling his or her call. If an evangelist or ministry leader is not raising up others, he or she is straying from Jesus' model. The temptation can be to increase one's own glory and not God's. The value of Spiritual Mentoring is to increase one's God-given capacities in a healthy, Christlike manner.

The concerns of Spiritual Mentoring are threefold. The first is *experiencing love*. When a mentee feels the emotional and relational support of the mentor, he or she is encouraged and is able to persevere more readily. So a concern of Spiritual Mentoring is to enhance a mentee's relational life. When a mentee experiences the abiding love of the mentor, no matter the suffering, the disappointments, the difficulties, he or she is often able to pull through.

This is what Jesus did for his disciples. He loved them to the end. He loved them so much that he laid his life down for his friends. Spiritual mentors, of course, are not called to lay down their lives. Jesus has already served as our Savior. But Spiritual Mentoring is not just a functional relationship in order to teach someone how to get something done. It is a fatherly or motherly relationship, as the mentor spiritually fathers or mothers the mentee. They do not replace parents but augment them, with a focus on the mentee's spiritual development. In Mentoring Communities, the mentee also experiences the love and regard of his or her peers.

The second concern of mentoring is *building character*. Building character is hard work. Paying attention to one's inner life requires focus, reflection, and accountability. We need others to come alongside and ask us the hard questions. When we have the positive regard of our mentor and peers, it creates a safe environment to be honest about our development.

I get depth from my Spiritual Mentoring community that can be experienced no other way . . . depth of insight, depth of joy, and depth of love. We bear one another's burdens and celebrate victories.

DEBORAH, LEADERSHIP COACH
(OREGON, USA)

While writing this chapter, I received two calls from two different people seeking advice about a ministry leader who had gone astray. One was a worship leader who took advantage of a church member. Another was a pastor who was living a completely unholy and hidden life separate from the appearance of spiritual piety he brought to the pulpit each Sunday. How does this happen? How can someone make a commitment to give their life fully to Christ, and then commit egregious sins several years later?

I believe the problem is a lack of accountability to pay attention to our inner lives. As noted in the previous chapter, the Lausanne Covenant describes character with the HIS acronym (which stands for humility, integrity, and simplicity). *Humility* is a character trait observed by others, not claimed for yourself.

Personality psychologists, who research the basic factors of personality, have recently discovered a worldwide factor of humility. For years, psychologists understood that the personality had five factors on a spectrum: extroversion, agreeableness, conscientiousness, neuroticism, and openness to experience.

These five traits were used to understand the human personality. They were universal no matter what culture or setting; every human being had these five traits on a spectrum. But then researchers noticed another large factor group, which was associated with humility. The spectrum went from honesty-humility to deceitful–self-centered.[4] Humility is a core human character trait recognized in all cultures. Jesus embodied humility.

Christians universally understand Jesus Christ as our Servant Savior. Paul beseeched the Philippians to be of one mind and one love, and that was only possible when they recognized that same mind came from imitating Christ, who humbled himself:

Do nothing from selfish ambition or conceit, but in humility regard others as better than yourselves. Let each of you look not to your own interests, but to the interests of others. Let the same mind be in you that was in Christ Jesus,

who, though he was in the form of God,
  did not regard equality with God
  as something to be exploited,
but emptied himself,
  taking the form of a slave,
  being born in human likeness.
And being found in human form,
  he humbled himself
  and became obedient to the point of death—
  even death on a cross.

PHILIPPIANS 2:3-8

A humble person is sincere, modest, fair-minded, and unassuming. Humble Christians are committed to glorifying God, not themselves. They are not seeking status or striving for success as defined by the world. They are not striving to be a super chicken but to be part of a community of productive, healthy people on a mission for God. A humble leader is also confident and secure in his or her adoption as the child of God. Humble does not mean powerless or invisible; it means being in service to a higher calling than one's own self-interest.

Integrity is simply integration of a person's outside behaviors with their inside nature. Jesus accused the religious leaders of his day of having a divided nature:

> Woe to you, scribes and Pharisees, hypocrites! For you clean
> the outside of the cup and of the plate, but inside they are full
> of greed and self-indulgence. You blind Pharisee! First clean the
> inside of the cup, so that the outside also may become clean.
>
> Woe to you, scribes and Pharisees, hypocrites! For you are
> like whitewashed tombs, which on the outside look beautiful,
> but inside they are full of the bones of the dead and of all kinds
> of filth. So you also on the outside look righteous to others, but
> inside you are full of hypocrisy and lawlessness.
>
> MATTHEW 23:25-28

The subtle temptation brought on by the difficulties and challenges of a ministry life is to compromise on your personal walk with God, on your inner reality of faith. The state of your inner world is often reflected in how you treat others in intimate or private relationships. It is the inner world that reveals the true nature of an individual, the true self, not the false self we create to present to the world.

If we are short-tempered, demanding, and self-centered in our intimate relationships with spouse and children but generous and warm in public, God is not pleased. Furthermore, if we appear kind and gracious to the people around us but harbor hate in our hearts, God is not satisfied with the state of our souls.

Anyone can fake an outer countenance, but it requires deep humility to stay connected to Christ for an integrated life. This is why we need mentors and peers who challenge and encourage us to have an undivided nature.

Simplicity matters in today's consumer-driven, success-oriented world. The result of attending only to those things that feed appetites or make you successful is an impoverishment of wisdom and a lack of ethical vision for the welfare of others and the environment. The church worldwide has been infected with a prosperity gospel that promises financial success as the result of faith. In truth, the result of faith is not success but love and service. The Cape Town Commitment addressed the problem of a prosperity gospel:

> We urgently encourage church and mission leaders in contexts where the prosperity gospel is popular to test its teaching with careful attention to the teaching and example of Jesus Christ. Particularly, we all need to interpret and teach those Bible texts that are commonly used to support the prosperity gospel in their full biblical context and proper balance. Where prosperity teaching happens in the context of poverty, we must counter it with authentic compassion and action to bring justice and lasting transformation for the poor. Above all we must replace self-interest and greed with the biblical teaching on self-sacrifice and generous giving as the marks of true discipleship to Christ. We affirm Lausanne's historic call for simpler lifestyles.[5]

Peers and a mentor can help guard us from the temptation to equate success with God's favor. Such relationships guard us from the belief that because of our faithfulness, we deserve to have easier lives than nonbelievers. Christians, especially Christian leaders, are called to lives of suffering and service after the life lived by our Savior, Jesus Christ. We aspire only to this: to be worthy to kiss the feet of our Lord.

The third concern of traditional mentoring is developing skills for fulfilling the mentee's calling, whether this is such skills as preaching, teaching, counseling, church planting, advocating for justice, or evangelizing. It actually is easier to teach skills, but it takes a lifetime of love to become more like Christ. Though the development of skills is an important part of mentoring, it is not the primary focus of Spiritual Mentoring.

Spiritual Mentoring gives full attention to the components of *experiencing love* and *building character*. These are the two most rare and cherished concerns of Spiritual Mentoring. Learning skills is not so difficult. Building character and creating an environment of safe people are gifts Jesus gave to his disciples and followers. Through Mentoring Communities with spiritual mentors and peers, we can give this to each other to strengthen our lives for the long haul of ministry.

Qualities of a Spiritual Mentor and Mentees

Spiritual mentors are people of humility, integrity, and simplicity. They are respected for their grace, wisdom, and kindness. They are prayerful and have a love of those far from God. They are proven ministry leaders. They are not afraid of the dark. They have suffered for the sake of the gospel and have become more beautiful. They have aspired to be like Christ. They are rare, actually.

My mentor, Dr. Leighton Ford, is one of those persons. This does not mean that he doesn't struggle sometimes or make mistakes sometimes, but he always comes back to the center: Christ. He always strives to be a better person. My friend Mark Slaughter, an evangelist, has said, "Two kinds of people walk into a room. One is thinking 'Here I am.' The other is thinking 'There you are.'"[6] Spiritual mentors are "There you are" people.

A ministry leader who would be a good mentee is one who is committed to Christ and to his or her calling. These people are teachable and honest. They, too, exemplify the HIS qualities of character: humility, integrity, and simplicity. Raphaël Anzenberger has said that mentees with potential for serving Christ—not themselves—"are called to be fishers of others, not keepers of the aquarium."[7] Besides HIS character, good mentee candidates have three other qualities:

1. passion for evangelism and mission—desire to lead *to* Jesus;

2. servant mind-set—desire to lead *like* Jesus; and

3. Kingdom-seeking orientation—desire to lead *for* Jesus and Jesus' rule.

When I want to know if a person has the right attitude and aptitude to be a servant leader like Jesus (and thus a potential mentee), I watch them. I don't say anything. I observe their behavior over time. I look to see three things in these individuals. *First*, are they responsible? When they say they will do something, do they get it done? *Second*, are they willing to serve? Will they take the servant position to help another? I once saw a highly respected university president notice an overflowing trash basket at a conference event in his university. He tied the trash bag, put in a new bag, and took the trash to the kitchen. He did not need to do this.

Third, do they want to act? Do they show initiative? If there is a problem or something that needs doing, no matter how humble, do they take care of it? Do they mobilize others to work with them? When I observe these things in a younger leader, I believe they are someone who would respond well to mentoring and who would be respected by their peers.

What Does a Spiritual Mentor Do?

My mentor is someone with whom I spend time in a Spiritual Mentoring Community once a year for five days. He brings a spiritual presence with him. He is genuinely happy to see each of us, and he makes himself available for one-on-one conversations. He leads us. He is also available to me throughout the year. We live on different sides of the United States, a distance of five thousand miles and a time-zone change of three hours. He will call me four to five times a year just to check in. He listens to me and he shares how he is doing.

If I am having difficulties and need advice and prayer, I can call him. Recently, I called him about a difficult leadership situation I was experiencing. Here is how it went:

"Leighton, I'm feeling very distressed about this leadership situation." I proceeded to tell him the story.

Leighton listened as I shared. He asked me a few questions. Then he said, "I'm sorry this is happening. Jeanie and I will be praying for you. May I pray for you now?"

"Yes, please." He prayed for me. A few days later, he texted, asking how it was going.

Leighton rarely gives me advice. Sometimes, I directly ask him a question, but normally, he is simply an encouraging presence. He primarily listens and prays. As a maturing leader, I do not really need advice. I need a safe person to help me be a better person. I need someone who will truly pray for me. Younger leaders sometimes need wisdom and some words of guidance, not to solve the problem but to give the developing leaders a process for approaching the problem.

Spiritual Mentoring is whole-life mentoring. Whole-life mentoring means that the mentor cares about the mentee's emotional and relational life, physical well-being, ministry journey, and faith walk. If one of my mentees is wearing down physically, I listen and then ask how they could better care for themselves. Then I check in to see if they follow through.

If one of my mentees is having difficulty in their ministry, I listen and ask what they need most. Sometimes, I offer some wisdom. I always pray for them, and then I check in. If someone is struggling with a difficult relationship, I listen first and then perhaps ask some questions. I encourage them to share the need with others, especially if they have a Mentoring Community. Leighton once said, "The focus of Spiritual Mentoring is to help people pay attention to what God is doing in their lives and to respond."

Mentoring Makes a Difference

The evangelist Billy Graham was asked what he would do if he were starting his ministry again. He said,

I think one of the first things I would do would be to get a small
group of eight or ten around me that would meet a few hours a
week and pay the price. It would cost them something in time
and effort. I would share with them everything I have learned,
over a period of years. Then I would actually have twelve ministers
who would in turn take eight or ten or twelve more and teach
them. I know one or two churches that are doing that, and it is
revolutionizing the church. Christ, I think, set the pattern. He
spent most of his time with twelve men. He didn't spend it with
a great crowd. In fact, every time he had a great crowd it seems to
me that there weren't too many results. The great results, it seems
to me, came in his personal interviews and in the time he spent
with the twelve.[8]

God called me to his service when I was a young girl, but I was trying
to figure it out on my own for years. Then I met Leighton Ford. He put
me on his GGTW list (Guys and Gals to Watch list). He began to mentor me, and my spirituality, character, and ministry field widened and
deepened, and I try to do that for others. I now have my own GGTW
list of younger leaders I am mentoring and praying for.

Space4Grace—My Mentoring Community

My group has been meeting since 2008. My group has couples and
a single person who works in Thailand. I met all of these persons in
various environments, but I realized they each wanted to do ministry
in community and to become more like Christ. The four couples work
in pioneer missions (mostly church planting) or frontline leadership
environments. Husbands and wives are gifted leaders and communica-
tors. They are very hardworking and are committed to ministry despite
difficult people, disappointments, and challenges. Each year, they look
forward to our five days together.

Lu, the person who lives in Thailand, works with Christian university
students of the Karen tribe. The students are first-generation university
students who have rarely been to a city and who live simply in the

mountains of Thailand with no electricity or running water. As children, they sleep in a dorm with thirty-plus hill tribe children while attending elementary and high school. The Karen are generally despised and disregarded by the Thai people.

Most Karen university students never finish their studies because of the isolation and stigmatization. Lu mentors these students in the Karen Leadership Development Program (KLDP). Karen university students apply to be accepted into the KLDP. When accepted, they commit to living together in an intentional community, going to university during the day, studying together in the evening, and praying and worshiping together each day. They stay together until they graduate.

Lu mentors the young leaders of the KLDP and provides retreats and spiritual-formation training. The program is free to carefully selected students who commit to return to their communities as spiritual leaders to help the condition of their communities. Her yearly travels to Space4Grace provide companionship and strength for the work God has called her to do, and she in turn creates a Mentoring Community space for young Karen university students.

In the end, Mentoring Communities increase capacity in two ways:

1. Personal growth in the inner world—it is easy to teach someone to preach. It is tough to help people grow spiritually throughout their lives, especially during hard times.

2. Connecting relationships—having an experienced mentor and peers gives people resources, support, and help over the long haul of ministry.

Bishop Joseph Likavo (of Kenya) lamented, "The lack of mentoring younger people led to the decline of many ministries in my country." Spiritual Mentoring is a fundamental part of Christian leadership and discipleship. Jesus mentored his disciples, and like him, we can increase the capacity and strength of today's Christian leaders by mentoring, particularly in community.

Safe Times, Safe Places, Safe People

Where Leaders Grow in Christ

My Mentoring Community has become a very safe and secure place to share my life, my brokenness, my ministry, my disappointments, and my joys . . . the still waters and green pasture of a busy year . . . an experience of Christian generosity affirming me in Christ and the ministry. Traveling with others, seeing them grow as they have been shattered by loss or delight in "success," we are friends, partners, brothers, and sisters on the journey.

STEPHEN, PASTOR/EVANGELIST (AUSTRALIA)

EVERY NEW LEADER believes they can make a difference where older leaders have failed. Yet when the reality and struggles of ministry press on developing leaders, their need for companionship is mission critical. In the end, idealism for the ministry cannot sustain the reality of the new leader's actual experience.

Often, after bursting out of the gate at the beginning of the race, the leader finds herself or himself alone, running around the track with no guidance for the next turn ahead.

As bivocational church planters, my husband and I were feeling the pangs of having very few people in our lives who could identify with our ministry journey and provide the encouragement and support of friendship in shared experience.

KARLENE, PASTOR (OREGON, USA)

Transformation for the long, taxing haul of ministry can happen when we are called into relationship with Christ and others in a Mentoring Community. We are no longer isolated and alone. We have others who love us and hold us accountable to the high calling of Christ.

Solution—Safe Times, Safe Places, and Safe People in Mentoring Communities

Over several years of participating in my Mentoring Community, I feel my heart has been woven in with the others of our group. Our time together is ruthlessly protected on our calendar and anticipated as one of the most restorative and spiritually filling things we do. I am grateful for the encouragement of these dear friends in years when I've been stuck in challenging situations and for their joy and insights in years when I've seen growth and opportunity. Their voices have been God's wisdom and grace in my life.

KARLENE, PASTOR (OREGON, USA)

A Mentoring Community is a yearly three-to-five-day-long gathering of a mentor and five to ten participants who leave ministry and daily life together to rest, listen, and pray for each other. Over the years, unique varieties of Mentoring Communities have emerged in different ministry settings. In France, for a two-year evangelist-training program, the participants are placed in Mentoring Communities with a mentor. Whenever they come together for training, they spend time with their group. They continue meeting yearly with their group after completing the two-year training.

In Mexico, national mentors are trained to create Mentoring Communities for pastors and other people in ministry. Each group takes a yearly retreat, but they also meet for a day either monthly or bimonthly. In Canada, the Mentoring Communities are an optional opportunity for pastors who are receiving special training from a coach. They come together for a week twice a year, and an extra day is attached for a Mentoring Community experience. The plan is for these groups to continue after the training. Internationally and in the United States, most Mentoring Communities meet once a year.

Safe Times and Safe Places—Going Away to Rest for a While (Mark 6:31)

In the sixth chapter of Mark, Jesus sent out his disciples. They were casting out demons, healing the sick, and preaching repentance. When they gathered back to Jesus to report all they had done, Jesus told them, "Come away by yourselves to a secluded place and rest a while" (NASB). This verse is sandwiched between Jesus' sending out the Twelve and the beheading of Jesus' beloved cousin John.

Ministry for Christ is a combination of wins, great disappointments, and losses. Jesus understood that when things were going well and when they were not, his disciples and he himself needed to go away by themselves. They needed to go to a secluded place where people could not find them and pull them back into work. They needed to rest.

God created us to rest each night and to rest on the seventh day. Resting reminds us that God is sovereign and God will accomplish God's purposes. The world goes on just as well with or without us. Resting reminds us that God loves us and designed us to need and want time apart with friends, family, and him. Unceasing

My first experience with a Mentoring Community was a turning point in my spiritual walk with God. A lot of spiritual warfare had affected me personally, and I was almost burnt out. My time with the community was powerful. I understood what it was to sit quietly at the feet of Jesus. I want to share Spiritual Mentoring with everyone. I understood it wasn't one more thing to do, but it would support me and give me life.

NYDIA, MINISTRY LEADER (MEXICO)

activity for good is the deception that we can produce apart from God's design and plan.

I have heard pastors say that if they are not working twenty-four seven, they are sinning. They explain that there is too much work to do, and therefore, to rest is selfish. They say Jesus said to "go," so go is what they must do. Yet God also said to make the seventh day holy, set apart for worship and rest. And Jesus said to go away for a little while and rest. Constant going is neither healthy nor worshipful.

Place is also important. We are connected to our environments, but we are often disconnected from the physical world. We aren't outside in nature enough. We are in homes, offices, buildings, and cars. God created a world that is good, diverse, and beautiful. When we are out in it, we experience God's grace and goodness in unique ways.

Being outside is a full sensory experience, and our senses of sight, sound, and smell call us to reflection and rest. Ministering inside buildings can also isolate our bodies and minds, so finding safe places in nature to be together to pray and play helps separate us from the expectations of our working environments.

> Our group rents a large guesthouse on a wooded property outside a small town on the Sunshine Coast of Canada, about two hours north of Vancouver, BC, by ferry and car. We gather from as far away as Thailand and as near as Seattle, but for all of us this destination removes us from our usual contexts and provides a sense of being away. The house overlooks a finger of water off a larger harbor and is surrounded with the beauty of creation. We hear eagles. We see trees and flowers. We smell the heat of the day and feel the coolness of night.
>
> SPACE4GRACE MENTORING COMMUNITY

There are three basic sabbatical premises for safe times and safe places. The Hebrew word for Sabbath means to cease and rest. The Greek and Latin words for Sabbath come from the Hebrew. Christian ministers and workers especially require and benefit from ceasing from their labors and strivings. They remember God alone is sovereign and God accomplishes his purposes.

SABBATICAL FROM RESPONSIBILITY

When a Mentoring Community gathers away in a safe place, they remove themselves from people in their regular lives and from their work. The place could be a retreat center or a house with outdoor areas for walking, meditating, playing, and exploring. Sometimes this is not possible, but having a place where the group is away from their home and work environments and where the group can spend daily time outdoors is imperative.

> I met with a group in the city of Singapore. It was the most central place for women from Singapore, South India, Nepal, and Sri Lanka to gather. We slept, ate, and met in a very small apartment that had beds and bunk beds, a kitchen, and a living-room area. We went out several times, once to see the city, once to a garden, and once to shop in an international marketplace.
>
> Four of eight women were the first Christians in their families; of these four women, three had Hindu backgrounds. When the other women introduced themselves, they began talking about their husbands' ministry and their children. Although all of them actively mentor women, only one of them had a female friend. Their time was consumed from sunup to late night caring for their families and others. The first time these women met, they were all exhausted. One had to slaughter, package, and deliver forty-eight chickens before getting on the plane to come. She manages several family businesses that support her husband in ministry. Another couldn't remember the last time she served herself food and ate off her own plate. One wept because one of the women brought her coffee in the morning. Another wept when she was covered up while she was resting. Though they were crowded together, with three to four people in a room, these

women felt incredibly blessed to have time with no responsibilities other than prayer and fellowship. They bonded quickly, and each one couldn't do enough for the others. They have met yearly together now for eight years.

Today, with the Internet, smartphones, and tablets, it is truly hard to take a Sabbath from responsibility. It is therefore important that when the group comes together, they commit not to do work of any kind, use social media, or leave for any purpose (other than an emergency) for the duration of their time together. It does not work well for one person to attend for a day or two and leave. The group commits to be together for the entire time without the interruptions of phone calls and online meetings. People usually check in with their families at the end or beginning of each day.

MERCY (SOUTH ASIA)

SABBATICAL OF TIME

A Mentoring Community commits to be together long enough that each person has substantial time and space to be listened to and prayed for. This usually means five days (arriving the first day and leaving the fifth day) for a group of eight to ten people. The core feature of Mentoring Communities is Group Listening Prayer.

This listening-and-praying practice is explained in chapter 10; for now, it's important to know that it usually requires at least an hour for each person. Each day, usually three people share and are prayed for by the group. If the time is too crowded, group members can tire from intense listening, and it becomes more difficult to listen to the Spirit and host the story of the person sharing.

Lon Allison, former director of the Billy Graham Center at Wheaton College, once asked a member of his Mentoring Community, the Point Group, "What do you think is the number one value of evangelical leaders in the US?" His colleague responded, "What do *you* think?" Lon replied, "I'd say it's frenzied busyness, based on what leaders talk about when we get together at meetings. Everyone complains about how busy they are. And if that's what we talk most about, it must be what we value most!"[1]

This is a sobering observation. Most ministers not only are overly busy but also lead distracted lives in a busy world. With so many devices and communication tools available, there is no longer a "workweek," with a beginning and an end. Leaders tend to be "on" all the time. Not only are leaders hassled by the external pressures of a busy world—and the expectations others place on them—but they also live with the internal pressures of addressing the issues of their own hearts. Mentoring Communities provide a sabbatical of time, both away from the external pressures and for reflection on the internal pressures.

SABBATICAL OF REST

A Mentoring Community commits to a schedule that creates room for the Holy Spirit to speak in the listening, the fellowship, and the joys of the place. To rest, one cannot be rushed or hurried. Resting requires enough space for casual conversations, one-on-one time with each other and with the mentor, sleep and play, solitude, group activities, and leisurely meals. To enter the sacramental space of truly being present to each other and to God, enough time is set aside so that there is no pressure to "get through it." Bible reflections and prayers are not rushed; rather, they are also experiences of rest and listening.

Safe People Who Create Safe Conversations—Listening to Each Other and to the Spirit (John 14:16-26)

When Jesus gathered with his beloved disciples before his arrest and crucifixion, he spent time comforting them. He was the one who would be betrayed by one of his own, then tortured and hung to die a suffering death on a cross. Yet he took time to comfort his disciples. He reminded them that they had an eternal place and that he would be with them always.

Jesus promised them the companionship and advocacy of the Holy Spirit. He prayed for them to be one and to love each other as he had loved them. Jesus did not expect his followers—especially those who would be at the front lines of ministry—to be alone and defenseless. Jesus expected us to be safe people who would create spaces for safe conversations together.

> As I experienced a safe environment, 50 percent of my problems evaporated. You see how the Holy Spirit works in the quiet moments.
>
> BISHOP JOHN, PASTOR AND LEADER (KENYA)

SAFE PEOPLE

In Mentoring Communities, both the mentors and the participants commit to being safe people for each other. The character of the mentors and the participants is therefore of utmost importance. Mentoring Communities do not work if the lead mentor or any one of the participants is more interested in building their own empire than in supporting God's Kingdom work in each other.

Jesus walked with his disciples. He developed them in their faith and service. He was a mentor to them. Mentoring is not counseling. A mentor is not responsible for "fixing" a developing leader's life by helping them sort out the reasons for their struggles. Mentoring is not just modeling. In other words, it doesn't mean just following a leader and watching them. A mentor is keenly invested in the mentee and desires to see them mature in Christ and be of service to Christ.

During a time of silence at a Mentoring Community training experience, I had a vision. I saw a broken walnut and found something inside. I received powerful words that I should be a multiplier of mentors in my generation.

ALAIN, MENTOR (FRANCE)

Neither is a mentor a parent. A mentor is not meant to become the family figure in a developing leader's life. A mentor is not financially responsible for a mentee, nor is a mentor required to bring the mentee into their home.

The mentor helps the mentee mature in Christ so they may become a more effective leader.

Neither is a mentor strictly a friend. A mentor must be able to speak truth into a mentee's life. Sometimes mentors see themselves as the directors of their mentees' lives, but this is also not the appropriate role; only God can direct a person's life. A mentor might notice things and make observations or suggestions, but it is not the mentor's role to tell a mentee what to do. Sometimes mentors like to have mentees so they can get things done that they don't want to do or don't have time to do. This also is not a Spiritual Mentoring relationship.

Mentors are experienced, proven, spiritually mature leaders who are God's Kingdom builders, not personal-empire builders. Mentors exhibit HIS character qualities: humility, integrity, and simplicity. They have a desire to lift up and invest in the next generation of leaders.

Mentees are committed to be in Christ and to become more like Christ. They have a desire to grow and have demonstrated capacity as people called into ministry, whether in formal or informal roles. They, too, have demonstrated interest and capacity to build God's Kingdom, not to create their own empires.

The posture of the mentor and the mentees toward each other is also very important to consider. Mentoring Community members are

- *Committed to listening*: Each is willing to listen with complete focus to each other and to the Holy Spirit.
- *Committed to transparency*: Each is fully honest about their inner and outer walk in ministry, family, and devotion to God.
- *Committed to loving each other*: With the same devotion of Christ to his disciples, community members commit to love, pray for, and hold each other accountable to holiness.

What if there are no mentors? In some cultures and in some environments, mentors are scarce or nowhere to be found. In these cases, there

In India, leaders are supposed to be perfect, so they have to learn to zip it and keep things inside. The first time in Mentoring Community, I opened up and shared, and it brought so much freedom and release. I was flying. I want India to have this. There is a crisis in national leadership because we are not bringing up the next generation.

MERCY, MENTOR (INDIA)

is no historical or ecclesial precedent for mentoring, which often means there is no word for mentoring or understanding of how it might work. Sometimes, the closest idea is *apprenticeship*.

In some cultures, the pathway from childhood to adulthood is marked by ceremonies, learned skills, or successfully completed tests. Usually, an experienced adult helps a child make this journey or helps a young person train for a particular profession. If you find yourself in a culture where there are few or no mentors, then create a peer Mentoring Community. Many groups have started in this way.

Michael Ramsden, director of Ravi Zacharias International Ministries, was prompted to start a peer Spiritual Mentoring group ten years ago. "I don't want to grow old without friends around me," he said. "Too many evangelists finish their life alone." He wanted a group of friends who could grow old together.

We were like-minded leaders, isolated from Spiritual Mentoring in our European countries. We shared the same heart and passion to see our continent reached for Christ. Andy from Spain, Christian from Austria, Kosta from Macedonia, Amy from the UK, Vlad from Romania, me from France. When we first met, we clicked. We shared our dreams, our disappointments, our frustrations, and our hopes. We could clearly see the benefit of journeying together for the long haul.

RAPHAËL ANZENBERGER, EVANGELIST (FRANCE)

SAFE CONVERSATIONS

In a Mentoring Community, another critical element is safe conversations. This means that any member of the group, mentor or participant, can expect that anything shared within the group is held in complete confidentiality.

- *Mutually shared*: The community commits to giving each person the same amount of space to be heard. Extroverts often find it easy to talk about their personal lives and their ministries, so it isn't difficult for them to take up lots of time sharing whatever is on their hearts and minds. Introverts, on the other hand, often find it difficult to express their inner worlds. The tendency is to give the extrovert all the time he or she needs and to skimp on the time with the introvert, since they tend to say less. In a safe conversation, everyone commits to sharing fully within equal amounts of time.

- *Private and holy*: The group commits to complete confidentiality. Whatever is shared is in a holy and confessional space. Nothing is reported to spouses, friends, or others. If a person wishes to share outside the group what happened to them personally during a Mentoring Community retreat, that is perfectly fine. But no one shares stories of what they heard from others in the group.

Safe conversations happen only when each participant knows he or she is held in

I was hiding. I was seen as a practicing evangelist, but the "self me" was hidden and there was no hope that I would be found. Because of the safe place, safe people, and safe conversations, I was found. I realized I was hungry and thirsty, and I didn't know it. My body didn't know it. It's like you go to the doctor and get some injections, and you get better, but you didn't even know you were sick.

JACOB, EVANGELIST (KENYA)

grace before the Father without judgment or fear of being exposed. If a person confesses sin, the group holds the individual accountable to make amends and change the behavior. The mentor and participants follow up with the individual to make sure they are following through. They will not report them to church authorities or gossip about them to others.

Some categories of confession require an intervention. If a confession includes threat of suicide or of serious bodily harm to anyone, the mentor and group must intervene to assure the safety of the confessor or the persons named. Ministry leaders do struggle with depression, and it is possible that depression might lead someone to consider taking their own life. The mentor is responsible for ensuring that the person gets outside help. The group and mentor commit to maintain a close connection to the person. Also, if a person confesses sexual or physical abuse of a child, the law requires you to report the person to the appropriate authorities.

Summary

Mentoring Communities are *not*

- social clubs or elite spiritual clubs;
- vacation times;
- training events;
- Christian conferences; or
- counseling sessions.

This is very different from counseling. When you are counseling, you go into your professional knowledge. Mentoring, on the other hand, is absolutely relying on the counsel of God. This is quite superior, and you can only understand it by experience.

PATRICK, PASTOR (KENYA)

Mentoring Communities are designed to create safe times, safe places, and safe people for today's leaders. God's mission is big. The work is too difficult to go it alone. These communities are all about walking with Christ. They are not just for fellowship and encouragement. They are not learning groups for developing theological insights or improving your skills as an evangelist or leader. They are not weekly small groups for studying and developing in faith. The focus is a lifelong HIS walk with Christ for the mission of Christ.

If they are from God, Mentoring Communities

- steadily increase members' love of God, self, and others;

- steadily increase members' effectiveness as leaders; and

- become a yearly pilgrimage with friends and the Trinity in an "away" place where Christ is met in worship, play, and prayer.

My Mentoring Community has encouraged me through difficult situations, life transitions, and general attentiveness in everyday living. It has helped to prevent burnout in life and ministry and has given me greater joy and a more thankful heart in my relationship with the Lord. It has also helped me encourage others in missions and ministry to consider long-term fruitfulness, spiritual formation, and care for the long run. I often think of Leighton Ford's life example and words of wisdom regarding a life of ministry: "It's not just how you start the race, but how you finish it that matters." Life is a marathon, not a sprint, and I want to run the race to the finish line, to one day hear those precious words, "Well done, my good and faithful servant!"[2] Spiritual mentorship is a gift to help us finish well with joy and the fullness of Christ along the way!

WENDY, MISSIONARY (MEXICO)

Mentoring Communities
in the Bible

Everyone needs a Paul to look up to, a Barnabas to be a
caring peer, and a Timothy to raise up as a leader.

RAVI DAVID (INDIA)

I HAVE ALWAYS LOVED God's holy Word. Even as a young person, when my life was difficult, I read the Bible for comfort and guidance. I didn't always understand it, but it drew me to God in a way I couldn't explain. As I grew older and had the opportunity to study in a seminary, my favorite classes were the Bible classes. I came to understand that God put into my hands his Word, and God put into my heart the living Word, Jesus Christ, and God put into my life the Holy Spirit, to guide me concerning the Word.

Whenever I begin a new journey or hear someone talk or write about something related to faith, I want to know what the Bible has to say about it. This matters to me, whether it is a theological idea or a spiritual-practice idea. I don't want to get entangled in things that don't matter to the heart of God or will distract me from Christ's mission path. So in this book on Mentoring Communities, I want to explore what the Bible has to say about such communities.

The concern for biblical fidelity is not just personal but is also the concern and value of the Lausanne Movement, in which we in the Mentoring Communities are involved in various ways. As noted earlier, in the 1970s, Billy Graham (an internationally known evangelist) called for a global gathering of Christian leaders and influencers. He wanted to bring evangelists together from all over the world in order to commit to unity of Christian mission and grapple with the issues of a rapidly changing world.

When the congress first met in Lausanne, Switzerland, in July of 1974, they produced the theological foundation for global mission with the Lausanne Covenant. The Lausanne Covenant is accepted as theological standard by as many as 85 percent of mission organizations in Latin America.[1] It was reviewed and revised in 2010 after the Cape Town gathering in South Africa, and it spoke of the Bible's purpose in this way:

> The whole Bible teaches us the whole counsel of God, the
> truth that God intends us to know. We submit to it as true and
> trustworthy in all it affirms, for it is the Word of the God who
> cannot lie and will not fail. It is clear and sufficient in revealing
> the way of salvation. It is the foundation for exploring and
> understanding all dimensions of God's truth.[2]

With my personal value for exploring all things related to life and faith through the Scriptures, and with the communal Cape Town expression of that same purpose, this chapter explores the biblical basis for Mentoring Communities as a spiritual and holistic tool for supporting evangelists and Christian leaders.

Biblical Foundation for Mentoring Communities

From the very beginning of God's Word, we discover an incredible truth. In Genesis 1:26-27, we read

Then God said, "Let us make humankind in our image, according to our likeness; and let them have dominion over the fish of the sea, and over the birds of the air, and over the cattle, and over all the wild animals of the earth, and over every creeping thing that creeps upon the earth."

So God created humankind in his image,
    in the image of God he created them;
    male and female he created them.

When God created us, he used the words "in *our* image, according to *our* likeness" (author's emphasis). This "our" is the first allusion to the Trinity. In the first book and the first chapter of the Bible, God reveals himself as expressed uniquely in community, consisting of God the Father, God the Son, and God the Holy Spirit (as the Scriptures later reveal). The fact that God created us in God's image means that we, too, are designed to be in community.

We can infer that because we are made in the image and likeness of God, God planted something in us that recognizes and yearns for a relationship with God. Being made in the image and likeness of God also means that we are created to be *in* community, as God is in community. This is our nature. This is not a choice; our very substance yearns to connect to the Trinity and to others. We are designed to reflect something of the nature of God. We are designed to be together in life and mission.

Community isn't some general instinct calling us to live life in proximity. It is a basic life-force that drives us to feel complete only when we are in community. We yearn for attachment with others. We want to know and be known. Anyone has the potential to be a partner in spiritual relationship with God and human relationships with each other. It can be realized in the marital relationship or in close friendships (such as that between Paul and Timothy, or David and Jonathan, or Ruth and

Naomi), but any relationship that reflects this kind of mutual support and closeness gets at this inherent need for our flourishing.

Jesus, for example, surrounded himself with disciples and called them friends. From that fundamental unit, the desire for community expands. Any time that we purpose together, whether to create a family, plant a church, or make disciples, God intends us to do it together. One of the great lies of Satan is that we can do it alone. The great lie is that we don't need God or each other. The serpent tempted Eve and Adam to go it alone without God and without a conversation with each other. Eve took and ate the forbidden fruit and gave it to Adam, who took and ate. They did not consider their choice together. The most fundamental chasm among humanity was isolating us one from the other. The outcome of this choice was a loss of partnership.

Some of God's leaders are convinced that they alone must be about God's work, that they alone need to be at the top. Some do not see others as partners but rather as workers to accomplish the leader's mission. When Jesus came, he refuted this deception. He lived his life in community with God the Father and the Spirit. He lived his life in community with the disciples and others who followed him. He went to the cross to break the power of the lie meant to separate us from the love of the Father and from our community.

The power of the Resurrection is a renewed vision of God's Kingdom in partnership with God's purposes—experienced together on the journey. God intends us to be in supportive communities. In those communities, we reflect the very image of God more clearly. In this book, we are proposing that Mentoring Communities can provide those opportunities for Christian ministers and influencers to be in supportive communities.

Commissioned by Christ to Go and Abide

God did more than simply create us to be in close relationships. When God created us and when Jesus died on the cross for us, we were commissioned to do God's work. In Genesis, we are commissioned to have authority over the earth and to care for it. With sin in the world, Jesus gave us a more focused purpose, and that purpose is twofold. We are set apart and commissioned by Christ to both "go" (Matthew 28:18-20) and "abide" (John 15:1-17).

> *Go* therefore and *make disciples* of all nations, baptizing them in the name of the Father and of the Son and of the Holy Spirit.
> MATTHEW 28:19, EMPHASIS ADDED

> *Abide* in me as I abide in you. Just as the branch cannot bear fruit by itself unless it abides in the vine, neither can you unless you abide in me.
> JOHN 15:4, EMPHASIS ADDED

Jesus commissioned his disciples twice: once before he was taken away to be tortured and hung on a cross, and once before he ascended into heaven and was taken away a second time. Both times, the disciples were confused. Yet both commands were given by Jesus to explain our purpose when he was no longer physically present. Jesus expects us to carry on for him, and he told us what to do. He trusts us to be his friends, in purpose and in relationship.

Our fundamental work is to "go . . . and make disciples" *and* to "abide" in Christ. One is active, requiring work, and the other is passive, requiring rest. Both are necessary. Both are Jesus' commands to us. Both are our urgent business, though I doubt that we give them the same amount of effort and heart. Mentoring and abiding in Christ go together. Mentoring doesn't necessarily occur in small groups and among friends.

Jesus came to bring the whole gospel to the whole world. The whole gospel is the Good News of our salvation. We can do nothing to commend ourselves to God. God alone is our hope and our salvation. Jesus alone is our rock. The gospel is not a "busy" gospel. It is not an "accomplishment" gospel. The whole gospel is the whole of who Jesus is and what he did for us. Jesus came to be the Good News and to bring the Good News. Thus, evangelists and leaders are to both *be* the Good News (by abiding in Christ) and *bring* the Good News (by fulfilling the great commission).

Most Christian leaders are pretty adept at the "going and making" part of Jesus' command. And of course, there are always ways to improve our witness and ministry effectiveness. We should continuously study and do whatever is necessary to be the athletes who run the race to win for Jesus' sake. Most trainings, gatherings, and conferences focus on the work of "going and making." All of this is hugely important and necessary. I have met Christian leaders and influencers who—at great personal cost and expense—have chosen to study or attend a conference to learn. This is holy to me, and I believe it is holy to God.

In God's eyes, it is not enough to fill our days with God's business, however. This is precisely why God instituted a Sabbath, a day set aside for rest. In the very fabric of creation, God ordained a day of abiding and a cessation of doing. The Sabbath is a day that we admit that only God is Lord and that he can accomplish his purposes in the world. It is a day that we recognize our humanity, humbly unhook ourselves from the machine of doing, and put God at the center.

I met a leader from Uganda who had been busy about God's Kingdom for ten years in a very large organization doing very important work. He confessed that he never took a Sabbath or a holiday and that he had never been present for even one of his children's birthdays because of his travel schedule. This confession seemed very tragic to me. We all can fill up our time "going and making." This is not hard to do because we begin to view our worth and status as emerging from our busyness, not our rest.

This is why I believe that Jesus publicly announced our purpose to "go and make disciples" but privately commanded his disciples to "abide." In the sanctum of their relationship, around a table, breaking bread and drinking together, he shared his most urgent, important commands about how the disciples were to go about mission. He modeled it with his life: Jesus often went off to pray and be alone, by himself or with a few of his closest disciples.

He expected, even commanded, that abiding in him was the only way to bear fruit. Being busy is easy; being still is hard. The command to abide is difficult. There is no external reward or value in abiding in Christ. People wonder what we are doing. People ask for an account of our time. Unfortunately, abiding in Christ is not as valued today as being busy for Christ.

The problem is twofold. We don't take the time to be apart with Christ, and we wouldn't know what to do in that time if we did. What exactly does it mean to abide? The usual understanding is taking time each morning or sometime in the day to study our Bibles and have Intercessory Prayers. But even those two actions can often become things we do *for* God, rather than simply being *with* God. In the later chapters of this book, we will identify silence, solitude, Listening Prayers, and Bible reflection in community as precisely those opportunities to abide in Christ. Mentoring Communities are places where we can be in safe communities, where we can share about our "going and making" but also experience abiding together and hold each other accountable for our abiding.

Connected to the Holy Spirit

Not only are we created in the image of God and created to be in community, not only are we commissioned by Jesus to "go and make disciples" and to abide in him, we are also given the Holy Spirit as a companion and strengthener for this journey. Jesus said he would not leave us as orphans; the Holy Spirit would come as our Advocate (John 14:18, 26). We have the Holy Spirit, who is in us, beside us, and among us. Jesus spoke of the Holy Spirit at his Last Supper (John 16:5-11), and the

> *I realized that mentoring and abiding in Christ go together. It's different from small groups and friendships.*
>
> DR. THEODORE SRINIVASAGAM, INDIA MISSIONS ASSOCIATION (INDIA)

Holy Spirit was poured out at Pentecost (Acts 2:1-4). The Holy Spirit was promised by Jesus and then poured out at Pentecost.

> When the Spirit of truth comes, he will guide you into all the truth; for he will not speak on his own, but will speak whatever he hears, and he will declare to you the things that are to come.
>
> JOHN 16:13

> All of them were filled with the Holy Spirit and began to speak in other languages, as the Spirit gave them ability.
>
> ACTS 2:4

The Holy Spirit is a real, active part of the Trinity, and the Holy Spirit is here now. The Holy Spirit is not a magical, spiritual being who came to earth for a few short years after Pentecost but a member of God's Trinity, sent to be God's presence for all believers. The Holy Spirit was given to believers for guidance, truth discerning, holiness living, healing, and prayer. At his final meal, with his friends, Jesus spoke about the purpose of the Spirit in John 14:15-17:

> If you love me, you will keep my commandments. And I will ask the Father, and he will give you another Advocate, to be with you forever. This is the Spirit of truth, whom the world cannot receive, because it neither sees him nor knows him. You know him, because he abides with you, and he will be in you.

In the first sentence, Jesus refers to the core commandment to "love the Lord your God . . . and [love] your neighbor as yourself" (Luke 10:27). One way that we love God and our neighbor is through the secondary commands of "Go and make disciples" and "Abide." First, we choose to obey. When we choose to follow our Lord and Savior and do what he is calling us to do, then the Advocate, the Holy Spirit, is available to us. The Holy Spirit was poured out on all believers, and when the Holy Spirit is active in us, we see what the world does not see and know what the world does not know.

Jesus promised that the Holy Spirit will not come and go but is with us forever. The "with you" refers to the Spirit's being among us. When we are together, the Holy Spirit is especially expressed as present all around us (Matthew 18:20). Jesus says we know the Holy Spirit because he abides with us and is in us.

The word for *abide* is the same that Jesus uses when he commands us to abide in him. Therefore, the same nonbusy posture is required to know and see the Holy Spirit. The Holy Spirit is quietly "with you," meaning right beside you. The Holy Spirit is "in you," making residence in the core of your being in the same way that Jesus is "in you, the hope of glory" (Colossians 1:27), the great mystery of faith.

In Romans 8:26-27, we read,

> Likewise the Spirit helps us in our weakness; for we do not know
> how to pray as we ought, but that very Spirit intercedes with sighs
> too deep for words. And God, who searches the heart, knows
> what is the mind of the Spirit, because the Spirit intercedes for the
> saints according to the will of God.

From these verses, it is clear that the Holy Spirit knows us intimately. The Holy Spirit knows our weaknesses. These are weaknesses of every kind—physical, emotional, relational, mental, and spiritual. The Holy Spirit can help us, which means "to rescue," as if we were being pulled out of the deep waters as we were drowning. Sometimes we don't even know we need rescuing because we are so busy and weary with life and work. Only when we stop and pray, when we are still and in a posture of listening, can we hear our inner worlds as the Holy Spirit is speaking to us and drawing us into truth.

The interesting connection between Jesus' final two commands and the Holy Spirit is that in order to know where to go and how to make disciples, we must learn first to listen for the voice of the Holy Spirit.

The Holy Spirit is given precisely for this purpose. We are not very good at this, however, for two reasons: (1) We are too busy going and doing that we don't have time to listen to the Holy Spirit, and (2) this kind of listening is done best in community.

Mentoring Communities are based on the biblical truth that the Holy Spirit is among us. The Holy Spirit is present in unique ways when we gather. The Holy Spirit is observed through the fruits of our pursuits, but the Spirit is heard best through humble listening and waiting.

The Holy Spirit is like the wind, neither to be seen except for the sensation of movement and neither to be heard except for the whispers in our spirits. We humble ourselves to pay attention to the Holy Spirit by abiding in Christ, by cultivating a posture of stillness—especially in community. Mentoring Communities can be places where Christian leaders and influencers gather to listen to their lives and the Spirit.

Biblical Examples of Mentoring Communities

Mentoring is an ancient practice found in the Bible and found in most cultures throughout time. Examples in the Old Testament include Moses and Joshua, Elijah and Elisha, and Mordecai and Esther. Sometimes the mentoring relationship disintegrated, such as the relationship between Saul and David. Sometimes a mentoring relationship was the very source through which salvation came, such as the relationship between Naomi and Ruth.

All of these relationships were used by God to further God's purposes among his people. The mentors in these stories encouraged, trained, advised, and loved their mentees. The reasons for the relationships were to raise up the next generation of God's spiritual leaders or to preserve God's plans for humanity. As in the Bible and as Jesus did, mature leaders mentor younger and inexperienced leaders.

From the beginning of his ministry, Jesus gathered not just one disciple, as seen in the Old Testament mentoring relationships, but a group of twelve disciples. Jesus chose twelve people with whom to live his life.

He chose them not just for carrying on God's work but for companionship. These were his friends (John 15:13-15):

> No one has greater love than this, to lay down one's life for one's friends. You are my friends if you do what I command you. I do not call you servants any longer, because the servant does not know what the master is doing; but I have called you friends, because I have made known to you everything that I have heard from my Father.

Jesus poured himself into his disciples and others who followed him. He prayed for them and with them. In special times, he taught them apart from the crowds. He sent them out to heal and teach. He rebuked them. He loved them. He died for them. When he rose from the dead, Jesus did not return to the religious leaders to prove he was the Son of God; he returned to his friends, his disciples—both men and women.

Jesus created a Mentoring Community with his disciples in order to multiply God's Kingdom work and be in relationship together. Jesus sent them out to make disciples, and he also had them abide with him. After Pentecost, the disciples often went out together in small groups. Paul had John Mark, Titus, and Luke with him. Priscilla and Aquila, a married couple, were a mentoring team. Throughout the New Testament in particular, we see the importance of these mentoring relationships for companionship and for effectiveness for God's Kingdom.

Committed to Serving One Another in Community— Acts 2:46-47

In the early church, after Pentecost, people gathered together in one place. From the very beginning of the church, believers and leaders instinctively understood the importance of doing life and mission together. At first, they believed that Jesus would return soon. When he did not and the persecutions began, believers scattered everywhere.

Day by day, as they spent much time together in the temple, they
broke bread at home and ate their food with glad and generous
hearts, praising God and having the goodwill of all the people.
And day by day the Lord added to their number those who were
being saved.

ACTS 2:46-47

Their understanding of when Christ would return began to change,
but they did not change how they thought about being together. The
primary image in the Acts passage is the image of hospitality, of serving
one another.

From the Old Testament through the New Testament, hospitality was a singular value of the Jewish people. Hebrews understood
themselves as strangers, not landowners. God owned the land, and
God fed and protected them. This central understanding of themselves as aliens and strangers in a land that belonged to God—and
of themselves as slaves who had been redeemed and called out by a
holy God—was expressed in the rituals of extending hospitality. The
head of a household would do for others what God had done for him.
Rituals of invitation, acceptance by the guest, and then feeding and
caring for the guest were part of guests' experience of generosity. The
host would always say that he did not have much to provide, but then
he would give the guest a lavish feast, as much as he could manage
with his resources.

The land shall not be sold in perpetuity, for the land is mine; with
me you are but aliens and tenants.

LEVITICUS 25:23

For we are aliens and transients before you, as were all our ancestors;
our days on the earth are like a shadow, and there is no hope.

I CHRONICLES 29:15

And you who were once estranged and hostile in mind, doing evil deeds, he has now reconciled in his fleshly body through death, so as to present you holy and blameless and irreproachable before him.

COLOSSIANS 1:21-22

Remember that you were at that time without Christ, being aliens from the commonwealth of Israel, and strangers to the covenants of promise, having no hope and without God in the world.

EPHESIANS 2:12

The quality of a person's character, their personal piety and holiness, was measured significantly by the quality of their hospitality. Therefore, Lot was willing to sacrifice his two daughters rather than give his two male guests to the brutal mob seeking to humiliate them. Lot's offer is abhorrent to us today, but few people at that time would have found Lot's behavior inappropriate.

This virtue was ingrained with the Exodus. God brought the Jewish people out of Egypt with a mighty hand and provided for them with food and protection throughout their journey to the Promised Land. When Jesus lived, he, too, came to bring freedom to people enslaved by restrictive religious ideas about God's generosity and love. By the time of Jesus, hospitality had become a way for people of status to enhance their position in a community. No longer was it about caring for the stranger.

Jesus changed the hospitality rituals. Instead of waiting to be invited, he invited himself. Instead of seeking the status of eating only with the "holy" religious leaders, Jesus ate with sinners and tax collectors. Because Jesus himself was a holy man, his act of generous love and grace extended forgiveness to his hosts. No longer was the guest being served. Jesus, the guest, became the host. Something of the nature of God's Kingdom is expressed in hospitality. This theme of hospitality, this image from Jesus and the early church, is a central spiritual image for the creation and value of Mentoring Communities.

Recently, I was invited into the home of a Kenyan pastor. I had met him in the United States while teaching a class in which he was a student. I was a day lecturer for a weeklong class on spiritual leadership for mission. When the students introduced themselves, David spoke his name and then said he was from Eldoret, Kenya. In a happy coincidence, I was invited to speak at an evangelism conference in Eldoret in a few weeks. David noted the dates, and then said he would like me to come to his home for a visit.

I didn't think much more about it. But several weeks later, when I arrived at the conference, one of the first people to greet me was David. He was not attending the conference. He was waiting to see me and invite me to dinner. We agreed on a night.

David came to pick me up at the appointed time. I didn't know what to expect. I noticed that he had recently cleaned his car, inside and out. I was touched by his attention to this kindness on my behalf. When we arrived near his home, he pointed out all the unique features, including a one-hundred-year-old railroad bridge. We drove to a point and then walked to the bridge. He was very proud of the old bridge, and it was still used by pedestrians but was very dangerous, with many holes. Then we went to his home. His wife had prepared a tasty, bountiful Kenyan dinner for me. His mother sat on the couch, with his little son next to her. I was treated with respect and yet, at the same time, as part of the family. I felt at home. David's wife gave me a necklace as a gift. *Who am I to be so honored by a person I met only once, in a faraway country?* I wondered. I was moved.

At the same conference, a senior Kenyan pastor talked to me after my workshops on Spiritual Mentoring. He said, "The Lord gave me a vision and I didn't understand it, but now I do." He was very excited. I asked him to explain. He continued,

> The Lord has given me this same vision over and over for the past two years. I felt urgency to obey this vision, but it didn't make sense. Now it makes sense. Now I know what it is. God

told me to expand my house, to build an extra extension that had a large room for gathering and some small bedrooms. I was to invite young pastors there for rest. I was told to care for them and to listen to them and pray for them. I had not seen anything like this, so I was confused. Now, after hearing you talk about Mentoring Communities, I know that the Lord was preparing me to do this. This is what I am supposed to do: I am supposed to provide a place of hospitality for young evangelists, to encourage and support them. Thank you for helping me understand.

In the Bible, hospitality meant being brought to a safe place, where you were cared for at no expense to yourself. As I did with David, you would experience the generosity of a host, which represented the generosity of God. You were the focus of attention, not the host. You were listened to and prayed for.

Conclusion

The Bible clearly reveals that God created us in God's image, to be in community. We are called to both "go and make disciples" and abide in Christ. The Holy Spirit is given to us precisely to help us with our weaknesses and to be with us, particularly in community. Hospitality invites the stranger into God's generous space. Mentoring Communities are places where Christian leaders can be in community, rest from their labors, listen for the Holy Spirit, and love and serve one another. Mentoring Communities include safe times, safe places, and safe people.

I am so grateful for the opportunity to connect with others in a similar ministry. It can be so difficult to find people to share with, people who have some idea of the pressures I experience, and I found this in Sustain. I hope I was able to be a supportive ear for them also. Being able to pray for each other in an informed fashion was so wonderful.

I had this image of our Sustain group. We were standing in a garden, around a tree we had just planted. It was a strong tree, as it had grown over the years and decades. It had a thick, brown trunk that disappeared into branches and leaves. Each person represented a branch. Over the years, when one branch was suffering, the rest of the tree helped sustain that branch, nurturing it until it returned to health. This tree represents our life journey through Sustain.

CLAIRE, MINISTRY TRAINEE (AUSTRALIA)

PART TWO

Essentials of Lifelong Leadership

Solitude

Written by Anne Grizzle

I heard a lot about solitude and taught a lot about it, but now I see it in a deeper way. I see how it can change us.

VIJAY, MINISTRY LEADER (INDIA)

MY HUSBAND AND I LOVE our three sons and the chaotic joy that filled our home as they were growing up. Yet we also loved to take time away, just the two of us. When family, job, and ministry made our lives so full, we had to work hard to carve out time for our marriage—every week, if possible. As hard as it can be to organize, if we ever get away, even for a simple overnight time for the two of us to be alone, it helps us reflect and renew our love. As much as we feel we are each other's beloved, for all lovers of Jesus, our truest Beloved is God. God must yearn even more earnestly for time with us, and he waits—alone, attentive, and loving— for us to come to him. Therefore, we respond by stepping away from all the things we do FOR God to make time WITH God. We follow the psalmist's cue: "For God alone my soul waits in silence" (Psalm 62:1).

In our Mentoring Communities, part of our role is to make space for God as our truest Friend. When we gather yearly into our communities, we eagerly look forward to catching up with each other, but what often takes us to the deepest places with God (and eventually, with each other) are the times we create for silence. Like a jungle guide shows us the soul of forest life, God sometimes uses silence to lead us from life's busy distractions to the heart of the Creator's raw love and beauty. After silence, the level of sharing in a group acquires new authenticity and depth.

For God Alone

Knowing and loving God is humanity's chief aim. How can we truly love if we do not spend time getting to know him? How can we love most personally and fully if we do not set aside time, spacious time with our Beloved? Time alone, one to one, is necessary to really get to know anyone intimately. Sometimes we avoid such direct encounters as too personal and difficult, yet such experiences are where "deep calls to deep" (Psalm 42:7), the depth of our souls to the depth of God's heart.

The psalmist does not portray this quest for time with God as gentle or passive. Psalm 63:1 reads, "You, God, are my God, earnestly I seek you; I thirst for you, my whole being longs for you," and again in Psalm 84:2, the psalmist says, "My soul yearns, even faints, for the courts of the LORD; my heart and my flesh cry out for the living God" (NIV). Though Mentoring Community members are eager to talk with each other, setting aside silent spaces—from evening prayer to morning gathering, or an hour every morning, or a half or whole day in the middle of the time together—allows our yearning souls to connect with God. Young leaders often are exhausted and need rest and spacious time with God. In my mentoring groups, the sharing that comes after these leaders have time with God has a different quality, for God has been given space to reveal and love and speak to their hearts. Group members hear deep yearnings, wrestling, and hopes rather than recounting of activities.

Time and space for this earnest seeking of our souls is a vital part of what makes Mentoring Communities refreshing and authentic. When mentors use some of their time with mentees to intentionally leave space for God, they emphasize that a mentor's role is not to give great advice or be an amazing counselor so much as to offer gracious space with THE Counselor and Comforter. Sometimes the best offering a mentor can give is to set the table by making space for God, whether it be a simple five minutes before talking or the gift of half a day with God for exhausted mentees.

My Soul Waits

Several years ago, I was led to live out—in a small way—Psalm 130:6: "My soul waits for the Lord more than watchmen wait for the morning, more than watchmen wait for the morning" (EHV). Each Saturday morning, I got up at 5:00 a.m., wherever I was, and sat in the dark with just that verse and intention before me until the morning dawn came. Before this, I had served God. I had prayed to God. I had asked God for things. But I had never really waited on God. At first, it was hard; eventually, it became the most luscious time of simple silence. Nothing was needed but presence. But after many mornings, a mysterious thing happened. After an hour or two of waiting, sometimes something showed up—an image for a poem, a person to pray for, a stirring in my soul. Almost always what came was of a different quality than my own usual "good ideas"; what came was from afar, in the heart of God. Several years later, I waited several hours atop a hill on our family farm before an idea arose as if right from God: Build a retreat home here. That was ridiculous, since we lived 1,500 miles away and did not own the land. But over time, that inkling of a nudge from the Spirit became the reality of a place for hospitality I would never have dreamed up on my own. Although the waiting was for nothing but God alone, the largest action in my life came out of a habit of simple waiting before God.

In an era of quick gratification and sound bites, waiting is not something most people like to do. Yet we will wait for a bus. We will wait to see a doctor. We will wait in line for a concert. Good things are worth waiting for. What is better and more worth waiting for than God? Willingness to wait without agenda or request or time frame places control and lordship back where it truly belongs, with God alone. Especially for leaders, the discipline of waiting keeps us humble, aware that schedules and wisdom and life itself belong to God. And waiting becomes a generous gift to emerging leaders, whose lives are full of busyness and tasks and missions, granting them a respite from hurry and breathing room with their Creator. We must wait on God when we have a critical question for discernment or need something or seek wisdom, but more precious is the waiting for God alone. This is the "one thing" the psalmist speaks of seeking, a holy gaze beholding the Lord's beauty (Psalm 27:4).

In Silence

Over and over in the Bible, we read of God calling people to spend time with him, to listen not for booming messages in public places but heart whispers in solitary spaces. The Old Testament prophet Elijah, worn out and despairing of his hard work as a prophet, traveled to Horeb, the mountain of God, where he went into a cave for the night. In the solitude of the cave, the word of the Lord came, asking him to stand on the mountain where the Lord was about to pass by. As Elijah stood there, the Lord was not in a great and powerful wind, nor an earthquake, nor a fire, but in the sound of sheer silence (1 Kings 19:1-18). Elijah's story suggests we, too, must quiet our bodies and souls in order to hear the voice of God. For our God typically does not come in a shout but sheer silence of presence—or, as some translations of 1 Kings read, a gentle whisper to that deep, inner space in our souls.

In an age of motion, it can be countercultural to "be still, and know that I am God" (Psalm 46:10). With our cultures today more full of noise and connection than ever before, finding silent places to wait takes intentional unplugging and seeking out a quiet chair in our home, corner in a church building, or rock in the woods. When we pause in our activity and busyness, we move from ourselves as center of the universe to God as Creator Lord. Centuries ago, Saint John of the Cross wrote, "God does not fit in an occupied heart,"[1] and "the language he best hears is silent love,"[2] and "the soul in which God alone dwells has no other function than that of an altar on which God is adored in praise and love."[3] This language of silent love is one that communicates across all cultures.

In any course on good relationships, communication is a key point. And the key in communication is listening. In the epistle by James, we are admonished to be slow to speak and quick to hear (James 1:19). That is with other humans. This is even more true with God: We need to quiet our own voices and, in the silence, listen long and deeply for the sounds of the Eternal. There are indeed times to pour out our souls, especially when experiencing difficulties, but sometimes the best approach there is also silence. God says to Job, "Pay attention, Job, and listen to me; be silent, and I will speak" (Job 33:31, NIV). Mother Teresa once said, "We need to find God, and he cannot be found in noise and restlessness. God is the friend of silence. See how nature—trees, flowers, grass—grows in silence; see the stars, the moon and the sun, how they move in silence. . . . We need silence to be able to touch souls."[4]

Silence touched my heart. Unless we just quiet ourselves, we can never hear God.

JESSIE, WOMEN'S LEADER (INDIA)

When I was twenty-four, I first met with a spiritual mentor. One of the things she suggested I do was take a twenty-four-hour silent retreat with God. I had spent lots of time reading Scripture, worshiping, serving in the inner city, and fellowshipping with others. But I had never spent twenty-four hours just with God. At first, it was a bit awkward. What was I supposed to say or listen for? How should I organize my time? Wasn't it rude to not talk to the people at the retreat center? But eventually I settled into a space of just being available to God, following the nudge to take a walk and soak in beauty, or open the Bible and let a passage nourish my soul, or simply sit in quiet, silently calling the name *Jesus* in rhythm with my breathing. By the end of the day, I had discovered a source of grace that would become a lifelong oasis for growing my relationship with God—times away in silence. My sister heard about these silent retreats and eventually asked her husband if she might have a day away while he watched their children. Not a believer in God or silence, he asked her why she was going away. She quickly responded, "To figure out what to do with my life." He let her go. When she returned from a soul-refreshing time in a simple cabin in the woods, he asked her what she had figured out. She said, "That I need to have one of these times every year for the rest of my life."

Steps into Solitude: Hush, Listen, Be

Hush

A kindergarten teacher I know gets the attention of a loud and boisterous crowd of children by quietly saying, "If you can hear my voice, clap three times," followed by a quiet clapping noise. At first, only one or two people hear her and join in, but as she continues that simple call, little by little, the whole room finally quiets and joins her until she can then say, in a low voice, whatever she needs to say. We must silence noises to pay attention to the great Teacher.

When we try to enter solitude, we usually have many noises—outside and within—that must first be gently hushed. Ideally, we go to a place that is quieter, without great distractions such as people coming in and out, loud noises, phones, or beeps. A retreat house could be ideal, but sometimes a comfortable chair in a corner of a quiet room or even a prayer shawl draped over us wherever we go can help us enter space with God. Of course, no place is totally quiet, so once we find the available place that is as quiet and beautiful as possible, we must learn to let outside noises go, like leaves floating by on a river. Susanna Wesley, mother of many, would pull her apron over her head to indicate to her children she should be left alone for prayer.

Just as distracting as outside noises are the cacophony of noises within: to-do lists, worries, shames, bodily discomforts. These can be even harder to hush. It's helpful to have a paper and pen to write down quickly the distracting to-do thoughts. Having something to help us focus on the intention of God's love can also help: a slow breath in rhythm with a word from Scripture, the flame of a candle or the sky on the horizon, the breeze in the trees. When distractions without or within arise amidst our quiet, we must gently let them go. One of my mentors has cautioned me not to be hard on myself when my brain keeps jumping to interruptions but to take each one as an opportunity to gently choose Christ once again.

Listen

We hush outer and inner noises in order to listen for God. Listening is an active discipline: We open our ears to pay attention to God. It is hard to really listen to people. God's voice can be even more challenging to learn to hear, not being out loud, physical, and as easy to hear as a friend with whom we are in conversation. Yet Jesus says he is the Good Shepherd and the sheep know his voice (John 10:1-18). How unique is every voice. A child spends a long time hearing a mother's voice and can pick it out anywhere. My sister Laura was especially close to our grandmother, for whom she was named. At a point when she was far from belief, when we sang my grandmother's favorite hymn at her funeral, Laura heard that peculiar, unique voice of our grandmother, mysteriously singing along from the heavenly places. We want to know the voice of God and the Good Shepherd. The story of the boy Samuel hearing a voice in the night illustrates well how we can miss the voice of God. He had to be mentored by Eli, who sent Samuel to listen for God's voice and instructed him to say, "Speak, LORD, for your servant is listening" (1 Samuel 3:9). Along with reading Scripture, taking quiet time to wait on God is a critical way to become familiar with the voice of the Holy One.

The Holy Spirit's whispers can come through simple awareness in our bodies, through remembrances of people that arise during our quiet times, through desires that show up in our souls as we listen deeply, and even through words from hymns, spiritual songs, and choruses that flow back to us. We must discern these spirits, weighing them with the counsel of Scripture and fruits of the Spirit. Spending time in silence helps us listen for God's voice and experience God's presence more personally. When we return to loud and busy places, like the children in the kindergarten class, we are more likely to be the first to hear the soft, holy voice of the Spirit among the world's noises.

Be

As wonderful as it is to receive wisdom, understanding, and vision, the real goal of our solitude is being with the one we love. Psalm 131:1-2 says, "My heart is not proud, LORD, my eyes are not haughty; I do not concern myself with great matters or things too wonderful for me. But I have calmed and quieted myself; I am like a weaned child with its mother; like a weaned child I am content" (NIV). A nursing baby seeks milk from its mother, but a weaned child just loves sitting on her lap, feeling loved. So often, we come to God with requests, seeking something. When we practice solitude, we are like a weaned child with its mother, just *being* with God, feeling his love and his holy gaze of grace.

> For me, work always came before God. I learned that God should come before work.
>
> ARNI, PASTOR (INDIA)

Rhythms of Solitude

In the spiritual life, we need to develop ongoing rhythms of going out and abiding, of ministry action and solitude. Jesus created a rhythm of periodic withdrawal: "Jesus often withdrew to lonely places and prayed" (Luke 5:16, NIV). This is part of what we hope to offer in our Mentoring Communities. A mentoring group that meets regularly and takes time for silence with God helps provide that regular source of refreshment. It can also encourage us to create personal rhythms of time alone with God.

Isaiah 50:4-5 suggests a daily pattern of listening to God: "He wakens me morning by morning, wakens my ear to listen like one being instructed. The Sovereign LORD has opened my ears; I have not been rebellious" (NIV). How good to start our prayer not with intercession but with being before God, listening for his whisper and noticing how the Spirit may already be stirring so we can join.

Besides long spaces for silence, small spaces can make a difference in the quality of our humility and listening. Starting any time of prayer (as well as meetings of Christians with important agendas) with some silence, even just a minute, puts God at the center as initiator. It prepares our hearts to listen, not just our mouths to speak. Finding small spaces to listen during walks or rides, while bathing or hoeing re-centers our souls. These rhythms of solitude keep us grounded in God.

Community in Silence

Gunilla Norris writes in *Sharing Silence*, "Silence is where God dwells. We yearn to be there. We yearn to share it. . . . And yet, in our present culture, silence is something like an endangered species . . . an endangered fundamental. The experience of silence is now so rare that we must guard it and treasure it. This is especially true for shared silence."[5] In our Mentoring Communities, the power of shared silence is a surprising discovery. The power of the pause, of silence before sharing, the power of pausing to listen after hearing someone share, the power of calling for a silent time together on the hill watching a sunset, or the power of silent walking together. One group I gather yearly agrees to spend most of the days in silence. People wonder what kind of community that can create. And yet, remarkably, the connections are almost more profound between people from simple offerings of prayer or a poem slipped under the door or a shared wonder at beholding a flock of winter robins or the design in a fallen log. I suppose that those who shared monastic community in Christ long ago and still today know this secret. But it is a secret blessing Mentoring Communities would do well to taste and see (Psalm 34:8).

My heart preparation for Christmas each year includes setting aside several days for a silent retreat. I invite others into my home to keep community but only those who truly treasure time with the Lord. We share heart concerns and prayers the first evening. We have silent group-centering prayer morning and evening and possibly also spiritual readings over a meal. Apart from that, we carefully keep silence to allow each one time with their Beloved. Over the last breakfast before leaving, we share what God has shown. One year, a friend discussed huge personal revelations of hurt and healing, of freedom breaking open in her core that God showed during the days of silence. As a therapist, I was sure that no amount of talking could have provided greater healing than what God had wrought with her in loving silence. Last year, one pastor said God had reminded her of her heart for Latin America, which had been cultivated during time lived there as a student. A desire to reconnect had arisen during the silence. I mentioned that I had friends in Bolivia with a mission whom I had also been praying for during our quiet and of course she would be welcome to visit. She said, "I'll go," and almost as quickly, around the table of eight, I heard, "I'm in," "I'm in," "I'm in." We were in awe at God's working through silence, sure that there was no way a week of talking could have planned this trip more beautifully. Nine months later, eight pilgrims marveled at the Spirit's graces during a visit to Amistad Mission in Bolivia.

Fruits of Silence and Solitude

The fruits of the practice of solitude are many. Solitude gives us a respite from rushing and refreshes the soul. It reminds us that God is at the center of the universe—not us. Solitude can usher us into our Creator's holy gaze of love and ground us in God. When we are silent, instead of just recounting activities, we notice deep yearnings, wrestling, and hopes. We can review our lives and God's working within them. Often, we realize God's most important direction for our lives during silent times of listening. And solitude can take a group to a new level of authentic sharing from the heart and connect people deeply in God.

Silent time with God often yields my greatest experiences of joy and intimacy, but it also bears other fruits. Once we cultivate attentiveness to our own souls and to God's voice, we can recognize God's voice even amid the busyness of life. We can create a quiet place in our hearts that we carry with us, like a turtle carrying the shell of its home. I notice a different quality of attentiveness to people in my work and ministry after my times of solitude. I bring a sense of peace and rest. I am more present to them and to Christ in them. Anyone who regularly practices a form of silent meditation knows the fruit is in the whole of life, not simply the silence itself. Silence grounds and restores us. I would even say it recreates us.

In mentor groups, we have discovered that when people are offered some space for solitude, they bring a new level of authenticity to their personal sharing. Indeed, some deep wrestling and dreams emerge, which are then brought to the community. One woman from my international Mentoring Community experienced a profound sense of God's calling while praying at a small bridge, which she shared in the group so others could witness and support that call. She returns to the bridge and group to reignite that call each year. Another mentee became aware of her deep ministry gifts and ways they were being squelched in her current context. Sharing this in the community afterward helped crystallize hard steps she needed to take to walk into the path God had created her to offer. Careful use of solitude within mentor gatherings is crucial not only to connect people deeply to God but to take a group to a new level of sharing from the heart.

Taking time for solitude in mentor groups is not only refreshment and enhanced time with God but also models a pattern that must be part of healthy ministry lives. Often, mentees realize in group time how they need to set up new patterns for when they are back amid the busyness, and the group becomes an accountability group for that healthy rhythm.

Mentoring Communities gather to ensure long-term health, spiritual vibrancy, and community for faith leaders. Solitude in the gathering provides not only immediate refreshment but a model for life rhythms and the fruit of a more peaceful, prayerful stance that ministry leaders need as they seek to be salt and light in the world (Matthew 5:13-16). Leighton Ford tells this story:

> At a Lausanne meeting, my longtime friend (the biggest car dealer in Charlotte, North Carolina) received a vision that little groups throughout the world were without a building in which to worship. He decided to provide materials to build churches where needed. Once, in South Africa, he drove eight hours to a pygmy village, where the tribal chief had two requests: that the church be visible from his house and that his son be trained as a pastor. When my friend went back to visit after the church was completed, he discovered that first thing every morning, the chief and his wife sat at the church for two hours. He asked him why, and the chieftain explained, "We sit and let God look at our hearts."

In Mentoring Communities, we sit and let God look at our hearts.

6

Prayer and Bible Reflection

Mentoring Community starts with Scripture. Our cultures are taught to submit to Scripture and its guidelines. It is possible that we can bring our cultural differences and allow Scripture to lead the way.

WILFRED, EVANGELIST AND PASTOR (TANZANIA)

EUGENE H. PETERSON, the pastor-theologian who wrote *The Message* translation of the Bible, noted that in the Gospel of John, the two primary verbs are *believe* and *love*. He writes this about the two verbs:

> When we *believe*, we respond embracingly to what we cannot see, the things of heaven. Belief is worked out in a life of worship and prayer to God, Father, Son, and Holy Spirit.
>
> When we *love*, we respond embracingly to what we can see and touch and hear, the things of earth. Love is worked out in lives of intimacy and care among the people in our families and neighborhoods and workplaces.[1]

Mentoring Communities are built on these two themes—*growing in belief* in worship, prayer, and Bible study and *growing in love* by committing to a community of fellow Christian leaders. In order to grow in belief and love, gatherings must include times where Scripture is studied and reflected on and where prayer and worship occur regularly.

Mentoring Community gatherings are not vacations. Neither are they opportunities for improving our skills (Ephesians 4:11-16). Mentoring Communities are gatherings for increasing faith and love in community. Incorporating Bible reflection and prayer into the rhythm of these gatherings, therefore, is necessary.

Bible Reflection

A couple of years after my stepmother, Lorraine, passed away from cancer, I was still feeling a deep, unsettled grief. She had been everything to my four siblings and me. Our natural mother left us when we were small, and we did not do well without a mother. When my dad remarried eight years later, we were ecstatic to finally have a mother, and she was wonderful. She made our house into a home. She was responsible for us coming to faith. We loved her. But several years later, she got sick with cancer, and we were devastated when she died. I had a lot of trouble returning to a place of hopefulness after her death. This did not shake my faith in God, but I still felt very lost. I began to pray for God to "find" me. I knew I was saved, but I still felt lost in the woods of this grief.

So I began to study Scriptures about the lost. I particularly focused on the three parables about lost things in Luke 15. I read them over and over. I studied them. I prayed them. I tried to see myself in them. Three things came out of that study. First, I understood that Jesus was speaking to *both* sinners and religious leaders. Both were lost. Jesus was not just talking to people outside the religious system. People who consider themselves faithful and holy can get off track with God. The religious leaders were lost. They thought they knew the way, and they had left God's way. And I felt lost emotionally.

Second, I identified most with the parable of the lost sheep. The Greek word for *sheep* was not for a lamb but for a full-grown sheep.

Full-grown people drift away from the fold of God's family and get lost. My feeling of being lost was not a worry about my salvation. I knew I was saved, but I still felt far from God. The sheep who wandered away knew better, but for some reason, she still strayed off (to find better grass, or perhaps she was just tired). She left the company of her peers.

Third, Jesus went looking for her, and he found her. I knew what I needed to do. I did not need to exhaust myself with worry or run around keeping busy to repress my grief. I only needed to wait in quietness because I knew my Shepherd would find me. I understood that God was calling me to wait patiently for my Lord, and I would be found. This was a profound comfort to me and moved me from a place of weariness to a place of quiet hopefulness.

As the lead mentor for the Mentoring Community Space4Grace that year, I decided to create a devotional and a prayer time around the theme "How the Found Get Lost and Get Found Again." So every morning during the week, we studied the parables in Luke 15. We discussed how leaders and evangelists might get "lost." I had each member of the group reflect on where or how they might feel lost, alone and far from God. When we prayed each morning, we prayed prayers of listening and waiting.

The Bible study that began our morning devotions came out of God's journey in me. As the Lead Mentor, I shared it with my group to help each of them find their home in Christ's arms. And this is my habit. Each year before I meet with my group, I discern which Bible passages might be most helpful. I pray for guidance about a central theme for our gathering. I listen to the Holy Spirit about what God is teaching me or shaping in me. Then I study and prepare short Bible reflections for each morning. This is the spiritual food that we consume each morning we are together. In the evenings, I have sometimes used psalms as prayers to close the day. Whatever a mentor might do with it in a Mentoring Community, Scripture is a part of the experience.

A Mentoring Community's practices are a distillation of the on-going personal practices of its members. The Mentoring Community is a means to an end: a curated environment and event that helps leaders not go too long without a meaningful comingling of souls and serves as an annual retriggering of essential spiritual practices for a sustainable ministry. The things done annually or monthly in a Mentoring Community reflect the priorities of members' personal discipleship and set the agenda for their growth over the coming year. We go to the Scriptures regularly as individuals, and we go to the Scriptures regularly together.

In Mentoring Communities, Bible reflection helps us combine the written Word with the Living Word, as expressed in the Holy Spirit, to listen to deeper questions in our souls. Using the Bible is not primarily about instruction, although that can happen. In this setting, it is a teaching tool not to help the group *know more about* God but to help us *know* God's work in us. Bible reflection in these groups is to be a door through which the Holy Spirit can engage each of us with what God is doing in our inner worlds.

Bible Reflection: Active Study and Listening

When we study God's Holy Scripture, we can approach the study in two ways: as active study and as listening. One requires our active engagement, and the other requires silence and attentiveness to the Holy Spirit. We are usually quite comfortable and experienced with *active study*. In active Bible study, we engage the Scripture with our minds and hearts. We might study by referencing resources. We take time to really unpack the context and meaning of the verses. We think about what the verses mean for us personally and for our ministries. We discern how to apply them to the people we shepherd.

Several times, I have taken a passage that I didn't fully understand but then studied it deeply, praying and listening for the Holy Spirit's guidance. I sought resources from other scholars to see what they discovered in their study of the passage. Eventually, the Lord led me to an understanding that would help me and feed my sheep. This is the work of a Christian leader and pastor, to study God's Word:

Ezra had set his heart to study the law of the LORD, and to do it, and to teach the statutes and ordinances in Israel.

EZRA 7:10

I will study the way that is blameless.
　　When shall I attain it?
I will walk with integrity of heart
　　within my house.

PSALM 101:2

One year, my mentoring group studied Jesus' temptations in the wilderness, and we thought about how we might be similarly tempted in our callings. One year, we studied male and female leaders in the Bible and thought about our own leadership challenges. Another year, we studied the role of people in God's Kingdom who are differently abled by using Dr. Amos Yong's biblical study on this topic.[2] We thought about how we tend to value our efforts and others through the lens of productivity rather than through the lens of being God's beloved children.

Because I love the early morning, one time I looked up all the verses in the Bible that had "in the morning" phrases. I found that we were able to study the life of Jesus and the early church through passages that have "in the morning" in them. These were active Bible reflections. There are endless possibilities. The end purpose is always to reflect on what God might be saying to us about our faith and relationship to God and others so that we lead more *like* Jesus, lead more *to* Jesus, and lead more *for* Jesus.

Listening is the second way of using Scripture. Our listening is based on the spiritual principle that only the Holy Spirit is the Spirit of Truth, and we depend on the Holy Spirit to guide us into truth. Our own study is therefore insufficient for understanding and seeing all that is true about Scripture verses. As broken human beings, there are times we try to justify our actions or thoughts or protect ourselves so that we look good to others. We need the Holy Spirit to reflect back to us what God sees so we can grow authentically in Christ.

Listening means that after studying a text, we also must let it speak to our innermost being by creating space and quiet for the Holy Spirit to speak to us. In Psalm 1:2, we read, "But their delight is in the law of the LORD, and on his law they meditate day and night." Meditating on God's Word is as important as studying it.

Listening to Scripture can be done by silently listening for several minutes to a Scripture passage. The pattern for listening is in three steps:

1. quiet ourselves;
2. listen to the Spirit; and
3. respond.

We *quiet ourselves* by not talking, by closing our eyes, and by making sure there is no distracting noise. We lay our minds in Christ's hands for rest and ignore busy thoughts. We keep coming back to our Lord, the Prince of Peace. We are in a holy space. We focus on the words of Scripture we have just read and/or studied. It is best to focus on a few words.

Then we *listen to the Spirit*. We wait, and this obedient waiting allows space for the Holy Spirit to stir our hearts and speak to us. Sometimes nothing comes. Sometimes what comes is expected. Sometimes we are surprised by a revelation, insight, or personal understanding. After we "hear" from the Word and Spirit, we *respond*. God always invites us to respond, either through worship, repentance, or a required action.

One morning, I was listening to Scripture on my phone, and a part of the passage read was Mark 11:25: "Whenever you stand praying, forgive, if you have anything against anyone." After the reading, I listened for what the Holy Spirit might be speaking to me about the entire passage. Then, very quietly, the Holy Spirit asked me if I wanted to grow or stay where I was spiritually.

I thought it an odd question, but I knew I had a choice to maintain or to grow. I said I wanted to grow. The Holy Spirit asked me again, and I replied the same way, but less quickly. Then, the Spirit said, *You must forgive.* And the Spirit brought before me, very gently, three persons who had betrayed my trust at different times over a span of twenty years. I was grieved. I didn't want to do this. It was too hard. After several minutes, I said, *I will do this; show me how,* and I began that journey. If I had not listened, I would not have heard, and I would have missed the opportunity to follow the Spirit deeper into the heart of Christ for my own wholeness.

There are several ways to incorporate Listening Bible Reflection into the Mentoring Community gathering time. Whenever you study or read a Scripture text together, allow time to quiet yourselves, listen, and respond. There should always be a few minutes for this practice. It is also good then to share what happened with someone or the group or to record insights in a journal.

Listening to Scripture and the Spirit is practiced in the ancient Scripture prayer tradition of *Lectio Divina*, holy reading. This brings together hearing the Word of God and listening to the Word of God. In holy reading, a leader reads the text while the others listen quietly with their eyes closed. The leader slowly and thoughtfully reads a few verses.

> This book of the law shall not depart out of your mouth; you shall
> meditate on it day and night, so that you may be careful to act in
> accordance with all that is written in it. For then you shall make
> your way prosperous, and then you shall be successful.
>
> JOSHUA 1:8

Traditional holy reading and listening to the Scripture has four steps, with a leader guiding the process. But people can also practice this pattern on their own. (I use it regularly in my devotional practice.) To incorporate holy reading and listening to Scripture into your Mentoring Community gathering, choose a passage that is not too long—four to eight verses. Then prepare everyone for the reading:

- **Reading God's Word:** Have everyone close their eyes. Say, "Listen for a word or phrase that you particularly notice as I read the passage aloud."

  After the reading, have everyone sit in silence for two to three minutes. Then say, "With your eyes closed, speak the word or phrase you noticed. Don't worry about others speaking at the same time."

- **Reflecting on God's Word:** Next, say, "As I read the passage again, listen for how the content speaks to your life today." Read the passage again, slowly and clearly, followed by two to three minutes of silence.

  After the silence, invite people to share: "What does the passage mean to you? What did you hear, or what are you feeling or thinking?"

- **Responding to God's Word:** For the third reading, say, "As I read the passage again, listen to how you might respond." Read the passage again, slowly, and have the group sit in silence for two to three minutes.

  After the silence, invite people to say a small prayer of response. Sometimes someone will hear profound, life-changing words, sometimes someone is challenged or affirmed, and sometimes nothing happens. All are normal.

- **Resting in God's Word:** Have everyone close their eyes again and listen while the passage is read for the final time. Say, "Receive the words and rest in Jesus' truth." After the fourth reading, the group might say the Lord's Prayer together.

  At the conclusion, the group might discuss their experience. What are some questions or insights? How does listening help us to see and hear the Word differently than a Bible study does? How might the group respond to these words from Jesus?

Making the Bible a central part of the Mentoring Community experience reminds us of God's story and our personal place in God's heart.

Starting each day with a passage of Scripture, some thoughts about it, and time to listen and reflect on God's Word gives the group common spiritual food and reminds the group that this is all about our devotion to God. Christ is our Life. The Holy Spirit is our Teacher.

Prayer for Mentoring Communities

Nothing is as sweet to my Mentoring Community (Space4Grace) than the first morning we gather for prayer and Bible reflection. We light a candle to remind us that Christ is our Light and the center of our lives. On the little table in front of us, we have a Bible opened to the Scripture passage for the day. Before we say or do anything, we enter silence together. Something holy happens when brothers and sisters who love each other gather around Christ and listen together, sitting in the holy quiet.

Jesus said, "Where two or three are gathered in my name, I am there among them" (Matthew 18:20). We often think of this passage in the context of Intercessory Prayer or worship. It also speaks to the wondrous way we experience Christ in the silence. We are not striving or telling. We are not distracted. Somehow, when we sit together in silence as a prayer, we are more aware of the presence of Jesus and less aware of our own needs. We sense our bond with Christ. In the stillness, we build the unity of the church.

There is an old saying that goes "People who pray together, stay together." I think this is true. It can seem impossible to stay together from our own human strength. We eventually separate ourselves from each other because of differences in theology, social statements, worship practices, and the like. There is always something that makes Church A uncomfortable with Church B and Believer A uncomfortable with Believer B.

Prayer reminds us that through Christ alone, we have hope and eternal life. Prayer reminds us that the Holy Spirit is the Truth, the one who guides us with the Scriptures. The experience of praying together knits our hearts into one. If Mentoring Communities are going to be together for the long haul of ministry, we must pray not only with words but also in silence.

Prayer has a central place in the morning, in the Group Listening Prayer experiences, and in the evening. Mentoring Communities are especially concerned with three types of prayer: *Listening Prayer* (sometimes called Contemplative Prayer), *Intercessory Prayer*, and the evening *Prayer of Examen*. The definition of prayer I like best is from Richard Foster. He writes, "Prayer is nothing more than an ongoing and growing love relationship with God the Father, Son, and Holy Spirit."[3] The result of true prayer is changes in our relationships and ourselves, and true prayer always glorifies God.

Listening Prayer: Contemplative Prayer

Our first posture toward God is one of humility and wordlessness. Our Creator God, who spoke the world into existence with a word, who sent the Living Word to redeem us, and who inspired the written Word to guide us, needs our devotion before our words. Prayer without words is a prayer of listening that gives God first place in our day and our lives.

Listening Prayer is found in two ways in Mentoring Communities. First, during the morning Bible reflection, or when we first gather as a group, there is silence. Often in the mornings, Mentoring Communities begin with silence to prepare their hearts and minds for the living presence of God. Listening Prayer is a prayer of obedience: "I am here, Lord"; "We are here, Lord."

Second, when community members do Group Listening Prayer (explained in chapter 10), they begin with silence again, to prepare their hearts. Listening quiets us. If we don't listen, we can stay on the busy highway of our own thoughts and neglect to wait for the Spirit's presence and guidance.

Intercessory Prayer: Response in Group Listening Prayer

James 5:13-16 reads,

Are any among you suffering? They should pray. Are any cheerful? They should sing songs of praise. Are any among you sick? They should call for the elders of the church and have them pray over them, anointing them with oil in the name of the Lord. The prayer of faith will save the sick, and the Lord will raise them up; and anyone who has committed sins will be forgiven. Therefore confess your sins to one another, and pray for one another, so that you may be healed. The prayer of the righteous is powerful and effective.

Mentoring Communities also practice Intercessory Prayer together. Besides praying the Listening Prayer together, we also pray for one another with words. Intercessory Prayer happens most naturally at the end of each Group Listening Prayer experience.

Intercessory Prayer is when we bring specific requests to God. It is especially powerful in a group setting. This doesn't mean that everyone in the group needs to use words. One person can particularly feel called to pray for the one who shared, to lift up his or her needs. The rest of the group might pray without words, lifting their hearts and minds toward God on the sharer's behalf. Intercessory Prayer is one of our priestly responsibilities to each other (James 5:16), so it is not neglected when we gather in Mentoring Communities.

Evening Reflection for Mentoring Communities: Examen Prayer
Anne Grizzle offers the following material on Examen Prayer as an evening reflection, a third option for Mentoring Communities to consider.

The Scriptures teach us that Jesus' custom was to go off by himself in the evening to be alone and to pray: "And after he had dismissed the crowds, he went up the mountain by himself to pray. When evening came, he was there alone" (Matthew 14:23). In the Psalms, we read of the psalmists' habit of meditating in the evening: "I think of you on my bed, and meditate on you in the watches of the night" (Psalm 63:6) and "I commune with my heart in the night; I meditate and search my spirit" (Psalm 77:6).

Another prayer practice of Mentoring Communities is doing an evening prayer of reflection. This reflection requires us to look back over our day with a spiritual eye, to remember where we experienced the presence of God and where we did not. We review our day. As sons and daughters of God, we want to be mindful of when we were aware of God and when we were not. God is always near and with us, but in the press of the day, we sometimes aren't aware of this reality.

The Hebrew word for *meditate* means "to occupy one's attention." Traditionally, two questions reflect the day's consolations (when we felt close to God) and desolations (when we felt far from God):

- When was I most alive to God?
- When was I least alive to God?

In the book *Sleeping with Bread*, Dennis, Sheila, and Matthew Linn simplify these two questions to two that can be asked of almost anyone, at any age:

- For what am I most grateful?
- For what am I least grateful?[4]

This is not just asking what I liked today but asking, *When was I truly grateful and most alive today?* And, conversely, *When was I least grateful and least alive?* When we regularly review our days spiritually, we notice that we are most alive when we are living out what God created and called us to be. What is true for one person may be quite different for another. I might love walking in the woods on a rainy day, and you might love sitting at a desk, intrigued by a math problem. I might come alive interacting with a young child with Down syndrome, and you might come alive helping organize a Habitat for Humanity build.

When we take time to reflect regularly, we see patterns that can guide our decision making and life choices and help us live out our truest callings. It is also true that our least grateful moments lead us to wrestle with our shortcomings, seek God for forgiveness, and compel us to more earnestly grow.

The Examen can also be useful for building Christian community. My husband and I (Anne) use it at the end of our days, especially if we have been apart, to connect our hearts. It takes us to what is most important in a relatively short time. The Examen can be used to connect in small groups or as a community, at a family gathering for a holiday, or with friends meeting for a reunion. And it can be a useful way to begin a Mentoring Community gathering. Often, at an opening dinner or gathering, we start by inviting each person to reflect on the Examen and then share. It takes us to the heart of our lives, so our speaking is more than just catching up on life events.

Group Evening Examen

What: At least thirty minutes for a small group of evening prayer with these questions:

1. For what moment today am I most grateful?
2. For what moment today am I least grateful?

When: At the end of the day.
Who: First five minutes alone with your journal, then share with your small group.
How:

1. Light a candle or place a cross or open Bible before you to remind you of God's unconditional love.

2. Place your hand on your heart and ask Jesus Christ to bring to your heart a moment today for which you are most grateful. If you could relive one moment, what would it be? Where were you most able to

give and receive love? What was said and done in that moment that made it so special? Receive the gratitude and life of that moment again.

3. Ask Jesus Christ to bring to your heart that moment for which you were least grateful. When were you least able to give and receive love? What was done and said in that moment that made it so difficult? Be with whatever you feel without trying to change or fix it in any way. Then give it to God and let God's love fill you.

Give thanks for the experience and share it with your group.

Alternative "what" questions include: When did I feel most alive? Most drained of life? When was I happiest or saddest? When did I have the greatest sense of belonging to myself, others, God, and my surroundings? The least sense of belonging? What was the high point of the day and the low point? What do I feel good about today? What was my biggest struggle? When did I feel sad, helpless, or angry?

Group Examen Modeled after the Wesleyan Class Meeting

Jason Wellman, senior pastor of a United Methodist church in Ohio, developed an Examen for small-group spiritual formation in his church. (Used with permission.)

We have invited small groups to move away from the curriculum-based, plug-and-play models of Christian education. Our version of a Wesleyan Class Meeting model allows small groups to take accountability for their own spiritual formation as they partner with the Spirit in this work. In each group, members share

1. *Consolation*—Where did I see God during the day/week?
2. *Desolation*—Where did I feel distant from God in the day/week?
3. *Testimony*—When did I do good in the day/week?
4. *Confession*—When did I do harm in the day/week?

These guided questions allow each participant to become aware of the transformative power of the Spirit, and over time, they allow the participant to see where they are increasing in Christlikeness. This transition has proven powerful and transformative for my congregation.

> The LORD is my strength and my song;
>> he has become my salvation. . . .

> This is the day that the LORD has made;
>> let us rejoice and be glad in it. . . .

> You are my God, and I will give thanks to you;
>> you are my God; I will extol you.
> Oh give thanks to the LORD, for he is good;
>> for his steadfast love endures forever!

PSALM 118:14, 24, 28-29, ESV

BLESSING

See that you be at peace among yourselves, my children,
and love one another.
Follow the example of good people of old
and God will comfort you and help you,
both in this world
and in the world which is to come.
In the name of the Father,
and of the Son,
and of the Holy Spirit. Amen.[5]

Listening

Written by Leighton Ford

*This Mentoring Group has given me the safe space to be transparent
about my personal life and ministry. The support and feedback have
brought direction, growth, courage, and a much-needed, annual
dose of perspective. I have formed friendships that span geography
and years with people who have a unique voice for speaking timely,
godly wisdom into my life. It provides a refreshing break from the
hurry of ministry life, a place where rest and renewal are valued.*

JOSH, CAMPUS PASTOR (USA)

I HAVE HAD TWO EXCELLENT personal doctors over the years. Both are
well trained and professionally competent. They are both respectful and
helpful. The difference between the two is in the way they listen.

The one would enter briskly, records in hand, go straight to his computer to sit down, then ask some questions about how I had been since
I last came. If I had a new concern, he would offer a prompt diagnosis
and course of action. But that was it. I understand, of course, the pressure he was under to see another patient every few minutes.

The other doctor does not have as many years of experience, but he
is equally well-informed. What matters to him is having time to be with
me as a person. He comes in. Smiles. Sits across from me. Asks how I am
doing. Remembers something we talked about before. Then completes
his professional tasks without rushing—thoroughly, efficiently.

They both care. But with the second one, I feel I have been received, noticed, valued, and listened to. And what a difference that makes.

Do you know what it is like to be heard—to have someone listen to you without hurry, without an agenda, deeply and with care?

What would it be like to go a lifetime without having someone listen to you in that way?

Once, I was asked to prepare and present a commendation for a good friend, who was being recognized for his contributions to the school where he served and taught. I asked him to come by our house and to tell me about his life—not only his professional achievements but the events and people who had guided him along the way, opening doors for him.

For nearly two hours, I listened, asking a few questions from time to time, as he described the people whom God had sent into his life. He told me of the two older women who encouraged him to go into ministry when no one else believed in him, of the very liberal church leader who had the grace to support him for ordination when others dismissed him as too conservative. At the end of the two hours, he told me with tears, "No one has ever listened to me tell that story for so long."

I was glad to listen, because I have had so many, men and women, who have listened to me across the years—my wife, Jeanie, and friends like our leaders in the Mentoring Community, who have helped me along through the darker times and have rejoiced with me in the very good times.

Listening doesn't only help others. A reciprocal, mutual blessing comes from deep heart listening. Those who truly listen find their own hearts stirred in the very listening to the other.

Mentoring Communities—the Call to Listen

At the heart of Mentoring Communities is the art of listening: *wholly* and *holy* listening.

The late respected management guru Peter Drucker asserted that the first leadership competence is the willingness to listen.[1] And in *Leaders*,

Warren Bennis wrote, "The leader must be a superb listener . . . successful leaders we have found are great askers and they do pay attention."[2]

Yet listening has often been overlooked as a key attribute of leaders. I remember spending time with several well-known leaders when I was young in ministry. After long conversations, I realized that I knew everything they did, but they knew almost nothing about me! They never asked a question. Starting then, I determined to be a listener to others—later, I made a practice of particularly listening to younger leaders.

If listening is of great value for leaders in any field, it is especially so for those of us who are sensing a call to mentor younger leaders who seek guidance while serving God's Kingdom purposes.

We are called to serve as a community of friends on the journey—followers, companions, and learners—together in the way of Christ. We are *followers* of Christ as our leader and the way home to the Father. We are *companions* with those who seek to lead like Jesus and to lead others to him. We are *learners* helping each other to grow in the art of Spiritual Mentoring.

If this is our call and practice, then we indeed need to become a community of "superb listener[s]" who are "great askers" and who "pay attention."

A central mark of our community is a commitment to help each other listen: to God, to our own hearts, and to each other.

Spiritual Mentoring is not a program, a technique, or a profession. It is an art: the art of listening to and with others in the presence of our holy God.

As the Celtic spiritual leader Aelred described times of holy listening in the presence of God, "You and I are here, and I hope that Christ is between us as a third."[3]

Spiritual Mentoring is a gift from God, for others—a gift of listening.

Like any art, Spiritual Mentoring is also a practice, an attitude of the ear, mind, heart, and soul. And we can learn through practicing the gift.

The mentoring ministry for emerging leaders is a time of listening together so together we may discern God's calling for the mentors and the emerging leaders in the great task of world evangelization.

God Speaks, We Listen, Then We Speak

The entire Bible is the record of God speaking in human history and calling on his people to listen. Isaiah provided this remarkable insight:

> The Lord GOD has given me
> > the tongue of a teacher,
> that I may know how to sustain
> > the weary with a word.
> Morning by morning he wakens—
> > wakens my ear
> > to listen as those who are taught.
> The Lord GOD has opened my ear,
> > and I was not rebellious,
> > I did not turn backward.
>
> ISAIAH 50:4-5

God wakes us first to listen, then to have a word for others. What is this word that sustains the weary? It is the word that is apt, right, timely, helpful, convicting, and sustaining. I think of many words that sustained me just when I needed them from friends and loved ones.

They came from people whose ears God had wakened and whose tongues God had instructed. In the passage from Isaiah, notice how divine guidance is offered not merely for our lives but to help our weary fellow traveler.

I know that God has given me this "word" at times for those who come for spiritual direction. I also know it has come from what I myself have learned and lived, especially through the hard times.

Our Model: The Great Listener

Our model above all is Jesus, the Great Listener. You remember his words about listening?

> The one who sent me is true, and I declare to the world what I have heard from him. . . . I do nothing on my own, but I speak these things as the Father instructed me.
>
> JOHN 8:26, 28

As the late Henri Nouwen described Jesus' posture,

> We will never understand the full meaning of Jesus' richly varied ministry unless we see how the many things are rooted in the one thing: listening to the Father in the intimacy of perfect love.[4]

Jesus listened carefully to others, as shown in his conversation by the well with the woman from Samaria (John 4:1-42). Having a conversation with an outcast woman, both socially and religiously, was unheard of for a Jewish holy man. Yet Jesus wanted to listen to her. He spoke powerful words, but he also listened. Jesus also blessed those who listened to him, like the servants at the wedding in Cana (John 2:5), the disciples who obey his commands (John 15:7), and Mary who sat listening to what he said (Luke 10:42).

Learning to Listen

One of our greatest needs is to learn active and attentive listening. I like to think I am a good listener, yet I have often found it difficult to listen attentively. This is true in part because when I was a child, my mother punished me by lecturing me, often and at length, so that I learned to daydream and let my mind wander. I have learned that listening takes much practice.

If we want to be effective servants and helpful leaders, we must learn to listen to God, to those close to us, to strangers, and to our own hearts.

Listening to our own hearts. "Praying is first and foremost listening to Jesus who dwells in the very depths of your heart," wrote Nouwen.[5] Every day, we need to set aside some time for active listening to God.

Listening to others. This is one of the greatest gifts we can give. When I listen carefully, with thoughtful attention, not to frame a reply but to understand, I am saying, "What you think and feel is important because God takes you seriously, and so do I!"

Listening in sharing our faith. Speaking skills are important in witnessing to others, but so are listening skills. An engineer described evangelism as "listening in on the conversation between someone and the Holy Spirit and speaking when given permission by that person and the Holy Spirit." As Keith Miller put it, when we listen carefully to another, it is like running our fingers around the rim of a cup until we come to a cracked place—the place of need—where we can help them to connect to Jesus.[6]

Listening to those we lead. As Drucker and Bennis said, the best leaders know how to listen. They don't just talk about "my vision" but about "our vision" because they have listened, and the vision is owned and shared by others.

To listen to God in his Word and through his Spirit—and to our own hearts and to others'—is crucial. Spiritual mentors must be good listeners.

So let my prayer and yours be: *Lord, teach me to listen.*

Why Does Listening Matter?

The God Who Speaks is also God the Great Listener.

One of my own morning prayers, one I repeat often at a certain time of year, is from Psalm 116:

> I love the LORD, for he heard my voice;
>   he heard my cry for mercy.

Because he turned his ear to me,
  I will call on him as long as I live.
The cords of death entangled me,
    the anguish of the grave came over me;
    I was overcome by distress and sorrow.
Then I called on the name of the LORD:
  "LORD, save me!"

PSALM 116:1-4, NIV

That prayer came to me in April of 2003, almost exactly a year after I was diagnosed with prostate cancer and a heart attack within a few weeks of each other. During those weeks, I cried out to the Lord.

A year later, fully recovered, I looked back and could say with great thanks to the God who listened,

For you, LORD, have delivered me from death,
    my eyes from tears,
    my feet from stumbling,
  that I may walk before the LORD
    in the land of the living.

PSALM 116:8-9, NIV

God Is Not Deaf

Deafness is a profoundly isolating affliction. Those who have been cut off from normal conversation by the loss of hearing often say they would prefer to lose eyesight rather than hearing. It is a choice I would not want to have to make.

But God is not deaf. Elijah taunted the prophets of Baal, saying their god might have lost his hearing: He told them to shout louder to get Baal's attention. But Elijah's God answered his servant with fire on the altar, and he is a God who makes the deaf hear, sang Charles Wesley.[7]

God is not deaf—but some days, I am! With all the noise of daily life, I may not hear. I need to keep in mind the great testimony of Isaiah, as stated earlier (Isaiah 50:4-5).

What a joy when the God Who Hears also opens our ears so we can say with E. E. Cummings,

> now the ears of my ears are awake and
> now the eyes of my eyes are opened.[8]

Getting Out of the Way

The best writing, speaking, and preaching come from first listening—to God, to others, to our own innermost voice.

But again, listening—whether to God, the other, or our own deep places—means that we have to get out of the way.

Madeleine L'Engle understood this. Here is her insight about the writer:

> When the words mean even more than the writer knew they meant, then the writer has been listening. . . .
>
> Getting out of the way and listening is not something that comes easily, either in art or in prayer.[9]

In John's Gospel, Jesus often spoke of how he listened to his Father. "Whatever I say," he explained, "is just what the Father has told me to say" (John 12:50, NIV). His words were healing words that led to eternal life. His hometown people marveled at "the gracious words that came from his lips" (Luke 4:22, NIV) and wondered where they came from. "Isn't this Joseph's son?" they wondered. They had heard nothing like that from the lips of his earthly father. What they did not realize was that he was listening with perfect attention to his heavenly Father.

This was true from the time he was a boy, when his parents realized he was missing after a trip to Jerusalem. When they returned, they found him in the Temple, sitting among the teachers, listening to them and asking questions. When his mother questioned him, he said, "Did you not know that I must be in my Father's house?" (Luke 2:49). And he was there to listen, to get himself out of the way so he would do his Father's will, not his own, and seek his Father's Kingdom, not his own.

No wonder Jesus' words were the most saving and sane words the world has ever heard. He had heard them from the best source!

Is it any wonder so many of our remarks are so inane, unhelpful, even foolish because we have not gotten out of the way. When we are so filled with chatter from every other source, we become deaf to God's voice.

Listening and Silence

For many years, I took my dog Wrangler to the woods and a creek near our house. It was a place where I was most likely to listen, to the moving of the water, to Wrangler barking at the birds. As poet Wendell Berry wrote:

> *Best of any song*
> *is bird song*
> *in the quiet, but first*
> *you must have the quiet.*[10]

With his acute hearing, Wrangler taught me a rule for listening: First we must have the silence, and not only the silence around but the quieting of all the inner chatter that preoccupies our minds almost from the time we wake.

Silence can make a profound difference in the way we listen.

Over dinner, a friend told several of us how silence has taught him to listen. Mike went with a group of men on a retreat to the Middle East. One day, the leader took them out into the Sinai Desert. He instructed them to start where they were and walk ten minutes, each in a different direction into the desert, and then stay there for several hours. At first, Mike found the silence almost too much to endure, almost terrifying. But as the hours passed, he found that his mind and soul sank into silence and eventually he entered a space that affected him profoundly.

"I was changed by this experience," he told us. "I am a different person."

His wife, Anne, was listening intently. So I asked her, "Did it really change him?"

"Oh yes," she said. "It did."

"How?"

"He listens to me," she responded. "Not that he didn't listen before. He tried to. But he always seemed to be thinking of how to answer. Now I sense he just listens to what I need to say, and I feel he understands."

Listening as an Open Space

My painting instructor, Sally, pointed out that in a good painting, there is usually a place of tension, and that this is ordinarily the place where the vertical and the horizontal meet.

I thought immediately of a fresco of *The Parable of the Good Samaritan* by Ben Long,[11] which is at a church in our home city. As I gazed at this with a friend, we realized that the "center of interest" in this work is the space between the eyes of the wounded traveler as he lies on the ground and the eyes of the Good Samaritan, who leans down to help him. That space between is the place of expectation and creative healing.

In holy listening, we offer a "space between"—holding between us a time, a space, which we empty of our own thoughts and preconceptions so that God may fill it with his presence. That "holy space" also becomes a safe place into which the other can speak, often haltingly, slowly, perhaps with some struggle, the tensions that they have been holding in, the hurts they have been holding out.

As Rachel Naomi Remen put it: "Our listening creates sanctuary for the homeless parts within the other person."[12]

Listening, Holding, Imaging, and Gathering

As we listen to the other person, we do not let the words fall to the ground or float in the air. Because this is "wholly and holy listening," what we hear is sacred and to be kept as a sacred trust.

So we gently hold their words (and also their silences) in our minds, our hearts, our imaginations. We hold them freely, until perhaps we see an image, a connection, that we can share; or we are reminded of a word from Scripture, or a voice that came to our own lives. This holding and gathering is a value added to the words that are entrusted to us.

One of my Mentoring Community participants, a pastor, came to see me personally, and he told me of the weariness he felt, the selfishness he often sensed in the church, and the way the gospel was often misrepresented. Cramped and worn down by those burdens, he was searching for a "spacious place." How would he describe such a place? "Not where everything is comfortable," he said, "but where the presence of God is real, and I can be fully myself."

I asked him to close his eyes and see what place came to mind. He thought for a few minutes, then told me about going to a spot on the north shore of one of the Great Lakes.

"From the shore, you can see for miles," he said. "On top of a mountain is an incredible forest, where I saw wildlife. I sensed the awesomeness of God. It was a healing place for me, just before we began a building program. It was like an Elijah moment, when the Spirit of God passed by. I was alive again, ready to go back. God was really there."

That was a moment of holy listening, when words of frustration, words heard, held, gathered, offered back in God's presence led him to a fresh visioning of his life and ministry.

Even as the disciples "saw" Jesus transfigured, so that the glory shone through, when we listen in this way, we are sometimes enabled to see the transformation that is taking place, the glory that is shining even through the pain and confusion, the hopes and longings being expressed beyond the present reality.

We may hear and see what the other may not be able to see and hear. As we open to God's loving presence, we are given faithful ("faith-full") ears: hearing God's voice beyond the actual words, and hopeful ("hope-full") eyes: seeing God make something out of what is not yet visible.

The Orthodox theologian Kallistos Ware wrote about artists, like Kandinsky or Van Gogh, who could compose landscapes that glowed with a "divine transfiguration, in which we see matter rendered spiritual."[13] If that can be true (and I believe it can) of artists who may not be aware of God, how much more true for those of us who are called to be—as Jesus is supremely—"artists of the soul."

Listening as a Sacramental Mystery

Listening is not a strategy. Listening is sacramental. In a sacrament, God takes something ordinary and uses it for his sacred purposes—as with the bread and wine of Holy Communion, blessed to us in the mysterious working of the Spirit.

Listening is not a device to accomplish what we want. It is an offering of ourselves to God and each other so God will accomplish his purpose. It is the kind of listening reflected in Jesus' words: "I come to do your will." "We listen to do your will." "I do only those things that I hear from my Father, that please my Father."

Listening is a sacramental space, where we meet each other in the self-offering gift of Christ and enable each other to listen and serve as we ourselves have been heard and served.

Listening and Waiting

Often, someone who seeks spiritual direction is in a time of discernment, waiting for a clarified sense of call for their lives.

And often, I will remind them that the spiritual guides used to describe "the time 'between dreams'" as a very difficult but also very important time in our journeys.[14]

I think of the "time between dreams" as like those middle-of-the-night times when we wake from a dream and everything seems hazy, and we're confused. We can remember bits and pieces of the dream, but not quite the whole thing. We wonder how it will turn out. And we are not quite sure what it is all about.

One of our main roles in Mentoring Communities may be simply to provide "waiting rooms" for our friends, and to be with them as they wait.

Our prayer may be for and with them:

My soul waits for the Lord
    more than those who watch for the morning,
    more than those who watch for the morning.

PSALM 130:6

In his study of T. S. Eliot's *Four Quartets*, Kenneth Paul Kramer cited a distinction that the philosopher Heidegger made between "waiting for" and "waiting upon."

"Waiting for" involves having a fixed and concrete result of that waiting in mind. . . . "Waiting upon" . . . involves allowing insight to emerge . . . without a prior desired result. Heidegger characterized this waiting as "releasement," and "openness" toward mystery that leads to a new grounding in that which is most meaningful.[15]

Waiting upon is the kind of waiting Mary modeled in the Gospel story. She pondered in her heart what the angel had told her about the son she would bear. She hardly could have known what she was waiting for, but she was ready to wait faithfully upon God to redeem her time, in his time.

For those of us called to be in Mentoring Communities, it is vital to practice waiting. This may happen in a spiritual conversation when a pause comes, when the other person either has nothing to say or is struggling with their thoughts, and we have no clear words to share. Then it is time to wait, rather than to jump in just to say something. Instead of being anxious about silence, we can allow it to stretch out, perhaps for minutes, while we quietly pray for God to speak, and wait for the Spirit to guide. I have often found that the most profound insights and directions come right out of such a time of silent waiting.

It may also be that our joining with someone else in waiting may involve weeks, or even longer, until the way opens or closes.

Wendell Berry, the Kentucky poet/farmer, has a book of poems from his Sunday walks into the woods and fields at his farm. Once, a younger friend in ministry was with me during a time of uncertainty and frustration in his ministry. As we talked, I reached for Berry's *Timbered Choir* and read these words to him:

> *To rest, go to the woods*
> *Where what is made is made*
> *Without your thought or work.*
> *Sit down; begin the wait*
> *For small trees to grow big. . . .*
> *Your rest is in this praise*
> *Of what you cannot be*
> *And what you cannot do.*[16]

My friend wrote these words in his journal, and for many weeks after, they stayed with him as he waited. And his waiting was rewarded with a new, quiet sense of direction.

Listening for Passion

A mentor who spends much of his time counseling and mentoring pastors told me of a session when he sensed no passion in the eyes of the pastors in his group.

"What are you passionate about?" he asked.

One said, "I have no passion. I am burned out." Another said, "I have some passion for people in my church but nothing left for those outside." Most were like that.

So he said, "Here's what we are going to do. I am not going to teach about it. I want you to take a piece of paper and go out and find some-place quiet. Then I want you to ask, 'Lord, what do you want me to do? What do you want me to do to find my passion?' Don't talk. Don't say anything to God. Just ask that question. Then be quiet and listen to what God says." After an hour and a half, they came back. Many had pages full. And many were full of energy.

Listening for passion! What a good thing it would be to do that: for ourselves first, then for others.

What Are We Most Listening For?

God is always calling us—down and up—on this journey of leadership. In Mentoring Communities, we are on this journey together and we are listening together.

We are listening especially for clues to the places where God is dis-turbing, wooing, or comforting, places of consolation or desolation—which indicate the Spirit of God is at work in ourselves and our friends on the journey.

I heard a gifted actor explain how as he internalizes the character he is playing, his body becomes a kind of carrier of the character. This could be an analogy for how we become carriers of Christ's image—through the Holy Spirit—when we open our minds and hearts to Christ's Word. As the poet Gerard Manley Hopkins wrote,

Christ plays in ten thousand places,
Lovely in limbs, and lovely in eyes not his
To the Father through the features of men's faces.[17]

As in childbirth, this process will be stretching and not comfortable but necessary to our growth. In our listening, we look for signs that God is calling someone to the next level.

When we listen, we are looking for clues to help discern the deep places where the Spirit of God is at work. These clues may be words or tones of intensity, anxiety, concern, movements of the body—eyes down or looking off, shifting, shrugging. It may be difficulty in finding the words to express thoughts, silences, punctuated perhaps by brief words or utterances. It may be emotions of fear, even hostility, perhaps facial expressions. And it may be especially signs and stories, meaningful encounters with God in prayer and Scripture, indicators of how God is calling, opening us to what may be next.

Who Can Listen Like This?

As Paul wrote about ministry in 2 Corinthians 2:16, "Who is sufficient for these things?"

With all the best intention and practice in the world, true Spiritual Mentoring—becoming midwives, as it were, to those in a spiritual Mentoring Community—is far beyond us. It is a daunting task: an impossible one, unless we remember that the friends who come to us are "letters from Christ," letters written not with ink but with the Spirit of the Living God.

As we listen, he is the Great Listener, attending with an attention beyond ours, understanding with an insight deeper than ours, speaking with a wisdom far greater than ours.

So we can listen with confidence because

I am encouraged and had a time of renewal and refreshing to me. My mentor listened to my heart's inner struggles and helped me to find God's peace and plans for God's work. It was really like God was listening to me, and it gave me fresh confidence.

VANAJA, UESI STAFF MEMBER
(INDIA)

such is the confidence that we have through Christ toward God. Not that we are competent of ourselves to claim anything as coming from us; our competence is from God, who has made us competent to be ministers of a new covenant, not of letter but of spirit; for the letter kills, but the Spirit gives life.

2 CORINTHIANS 3:4-6

I end with a prayer written by Dr. Lloyd Ogilvie, which I have used for many years as I prepare to preach or begin some other ministry.

A PRAYER BEFORE ENTERING INTO THE MINISTRY OF LISTENING
Lord, here's my mind, think your thoughts in me.
Be my wisdom, knowledge, and insight.
Here is my voice.
You told me not to worry what to say and how to say it.
Free me to speak with silence or words, whichever is needed.
Give me your timing and tenderness.
Now Lord, here is my body.
Release creative affection in my face, my touch, my embrace.
And Christ, if there is something I am to do by your indwelling presence,
however menial or tough, control my will to do it.
Lord, I am ready now to be your manifest intervention in situations,
to infuse joy, or absorb pain and aching anguish.
I plan to live this day and the rest of my life in the reality of you in me.
Thank you for making it so![18]

Questions

Waiting is a fertile ground for questions.
ANNE ZAKI (EGYPT)

I HAVE A FRIEND, PAUL, who went to his spiritual director's office for conversation once a month.[1] After almost a year of these monthly, hour-long visits, Paul noticed a beautiful wooden duck sitting on the shelf of his director's bookcase. The book case and the shelf with the duck on it were in plain view, directly behind where his director always sat, but Paul hadn't seen it before.

He said, "Oh, I see you have a wooden duck on your bookshelf! Is it new? It looks so real." The director replied, "No, it's always been there. I received it several years ago, as a gift." Paul couldn't believe he hadn't noticed it before. But Paul's experience is not unique. Many of us miss seeing obvious things in our lives, even things as beautiful as the wooden duck.

The benefit of spiritual companions is often "seeing" something in each other that matters but that has gone unnoticed. The story of my friend Paul's noticing the duck illustrates the benefit of Mentoring Communities. The mentor and peer companions help each other to "notice the duck," observe one another's inner world and the mysterious activity of God, which can go unnoticed. Our busyness and non-reflective lifestyles can mask the obvious.

The mentor and Mentoring Community friends look over the bookshelves of each other's lives, searching for ducks. Finding a duck is not always easy, but one way to reveal it is to ask questions. Questions are a tool for helping people notice what might otherwise be overlooked. For sure, questions are a tool for getting to know one another well. Asking questions is an invitation to know and to be known.

Asking questions is like asking to be invited into someone's house as a guest. Think of our personhood, our inner selves, like a house. Anyone can see our outward physical presence and know a little something about who we are. Male or female, old or young, married or not, ethnicity, emotional and mental health (depressed, peaceful, content, driven), sometimes even culture or economic status—all these are usually discernible from the outside.

When we ask each other questions, we are asking to know each other more deeply. Each question is like a knock on the door of our inner house. Questions invite each listener—mentor and/or Mentoring Community companions—into the inner world of another, beyond the presented self.

The presented self is sometimes referred to as the false self, because it presents to the world a construction of what we think we're supposed to be based on the world's ambitions or what we want people to see because of our fear and insecurities. For Mentoring Communities to work well, we must present our true selves. This is not easy. Therefore, we need mentors and friends we trust in community to ask each other questions, so that we all might be truly known and fully grow into the image of Christ in us.

Asking spiritual questions of each other moves us from the outside of the house to the inside. We know that on the inside, the Holy Spirit is not content to sit on the couch and be polite. The Holy Spirit wants to go into all the recesses, closets, boxes, and storage places of our inner house. There, with the light of Christ, we might begin a journey toward authenticity and wholeness in Christ. We need each other in order to do this well.

Spiritual companionship in Mentoring Communities first requires us to listen well, as stated in the previous chapter. We listen to the person responding to a question while also seeking the guidance of the Holy Spirit. It requires a creative attentiveness to the process. As companions on the journey, we impose no expectations or agenda on each other, beyond believing that God is present, loves us, and is calling us into deeper understandings of ourselves and of our Lord.

The questions themselves are *spiritual* because we are not doing therapy or discipling each other toward a particular understanding of the spiritual life.[2] We are not trying to teach doctrine or fix a relationship or resolve a crisis. We ask questions to discover where God is moving in each other's lives. We are looking for the duck in each other.

In Mentoring Communities, we serve as spiritual companions to each other. A companion's responsibility is to create a space for grace, so that in the experience of sharing, a person finds his or her own truth. Having a safe, grace-filled environment in which to give voice to the inner stirrings and doubts of one's soul is profound. At the same time, we are infinitely able to hide from ourselves and deceive ourselves into accepting some truth that might be a distortion of our true selves. Therefore, questions can sometimes nudge a person toward more awareness, or even open her or him to an avenue of thought not previously considered. Jesus himself asked lots of questions and serves as a model for the usefulness of questions during spiritual conversations.

Jesus: Master of the Questions

The Gospels are replete with questions that people asked Jesus and vice versa. Jesus understood the power of the question to get beneath the surface and reveal the primary issues. He often asked a question before acting or responded to a question with a question. Jesus used two basic types: *rhetorical questions* and *invitation questions*. Rhetorical questions are those for which no answer is expected. The answer is obvious and thus remains unspoken. In the Gospels, the correct answers to Jesus' rhetorical questions often exposed the hypocrisy of the religious leaders. An example is found in Luke 14:3-6:

> Jesus asked the lawyers and Pharisees, "Is it lawful to cure people on the sabbath, or not?" But they were silent. So Jesus took him [a man suffering from dropsy] and healed him, and sent him away. Then he said to them, "If one of you has a child or an ox that has fallen into a well, will you not immediately pull it out on a sabbath day?" And they could not reply to this.

With the second type, invitation questions, an answer is expected. Jesus used such questions to probe motives or invite someone to speak their desire. This type illustrates the potential of questions to uncover what is less obvious or what needs to be given voice. The story of the lawyer in Luke 10:25-28 illustrates this type of question:

> Just then a lawyer stood up to test Jesus. "Teacher," he said, "what must I do to inherit eternal life?" He said to him, "What is written in the law? What do you read there?" He answered, "You shall love the Lord your God with all your heart, and with all your soul, and with all your strength, and with all your mind; and your neighbor as yourself." And he said to him, "You have given the right answer; do this, and you will live."

Instead of answering the lawyer's question, Jesus asked him a question. He turned the focus back on the lawyer, effectively defusing his attempt to trap Jesus. Then Jesus used the lawyer's answer as his own. Jesus went on to teach the crowd the amazing-grace story of the Good Samaritan.

Sometimes we ask questions to keep the attention focused on some-one else, not ourselves. In Mentoring Communities, especially at the beginning, group members might be nervous, be polite, or avoid shar-ing. On these occasions, it is the mentor's role to flip the question back rather than answering. It is a gift of hospitality; the time is returned to the one whose turn it is to share. Sometimes, people give short answers, so asking more questions can lead to clearer understanding.

Another example of an invitation question is found in Luke 9:18-20, when Jesus asked the disciples about his identity. He asked an easier ques-tion first, followed by a harder one.

> Once when Jesus was praying alone, with only the disciples near
> him, he asked them, "Who do the crowds say that I am?" They
> answered, "John the Baptist; but others, Elijah; and still others,
> that one of the ancient prophets has arisen." He said to them,
> "But who do you say that I am?" Peter answered, "The Messiah of
> God."

The art of asking spiritual questions is often precisely this: going from one question to another like stepping-stones, allowing the Holy Spirit to uncover God's movements.

The ease with which Jesus engaged people with questions bears wit-ness to the clarity of his calling. Hostility did not distract him or lead him to self-doubt. If the disciples or crowd were confused, he did not try to pacify them. He didn't need to prove himself worthy of their devotion. Neither was he afraid. Jesus brought his full attention to the concerns and needs of those before him. As Mentoring Community companions, we have the same responsibility to bring our full attention to those before us without internal distractions.

Barriers to Asking Spirit-Led Questions

In spiritual companionship, the listening process moves between attend-ing to the person sharing and the people listening. The listeners are not in a pristine, uninvolved state. When we open ourselves to the Holy Spirit while hosting the journey-telling of another person, we can become either a door or a barrier to the process. We are a door when we stay in a listening-hosting posture, paying attention to our own thoughts and movements but not being absorbed by them. We are a barrier when we become distracted by what is going on in our minds or with our emotions.

Paying attention to our internal activity as listeners is necessary. Monitoring our own thoughts and emotions while listening to the person sharing and the Holy Spirit requires a great deal of focus and self-awareness. If we find ourselves thinking about ourselves, not the Spirit, we have drifted.

A way to continue listening and paying attention to the person sharing is holding them before Christ and focusing on Christ's presence and the presence of the person sharing. If we begin thinking of other things besides the person's words, we push the personal musings and thoughts by allowing them to pass, like a car going by on the street. This is why silence is important: It trains us to attend primarily to God and others.

Three attitudes can distract us from listening well. And when we get distracted, we are unable to ask good questions. When these attitudes get in the way, we see only ourselves and not the duck. They are

- Arrogance
- Fear
- Impatience

Arrogance is evident when, while listening to another's story, we quickly move to a conclusion and consider how to frame our response. It happens when we assume that we know what is going on in the person sharing. We've had a similar experience, and we have a Scripture verse or a teaching to share. When we assume an arrogant posture, we believe we know the answer. There is no deep listening.

With arrogance, sometimes we ask leading questions to get a person right where we want them. We do not listen because we have already drawn our conclusion. Such thoughts act as a barrier to the Holy Spirit and to the person discovering their own truth. There is a difference between our assumption about the truth and a word of Truth from the Holy Spirit.

We discern the difference by testing our own spirit. The test is this: If we feel pride, a sense of rightness, or hurry, we are experiencing a spirit of arrogance. If there is no personal feeling of pride or hurry, the door remains open for the movement of God. If we are absorbed in our own thoughts and how they might be framed, that is a spirit of arrogance. When we listen to the Holy Spirit rather than make assumptions, a question might arise rather than an answer.

Fear is the opposite of arrogance. Instead of rushing forward with knowledge, we rush away internally with anxiety. This happens when a person shares something that overwhelms us. We feel "out of our league," so to speak. Sometimes when someone shares, we are triggered by our own pain and journey, and we can't listen anymore.

I have discovered that as soon as I get anxious about what to say or do next, I've shut the door to the Holy Spirit and the person in front of me. One of the primary disciplines of a spiritual companion and mentor is to stay centered and focused on that person. If we cannot, it is rarely possible to listen for the questions. As soon as we focus on our own fears, we lose connection with the Holy Spirit. If this happens, the listener must try to return their focus back to the individual. In attentive listening, sometimes a question comes.

The third barrier is *impatience*. Sometimes we wish people would just get to the point. We hear so much; sometimes it's hard to be completely present with someone going over the same problems we've heard many times before. It's obvious to us, so why don't they figure it out or get over it?

It's interesting how often Jesus simply let people be where they were. He didn't warn them that they were going to perish, tell them that they were completely off base, or hurry them to get it together. He let them be responsible for their own journeys. This does not mean that we don't ask probing questions about a person's condition or that we don't hold them accountable. It does mean that the Spirit leads the process, not us. Our responsibility is to give people space to settle into their souls. A question can stimulate reflection, but if we hurry people, they feel shut down.

Being self-aware while simultaneously remaining attentive to the other allows us to be in the optimal space for when and how to ask questions. I will suggest different types of questions, but keep in mind that it's necessary to listen to the Holy Spirit to know which ones to ask in a given situation (the Spirit might even lead you to ask different questions than the types listed below).

Types of Questions

A family story is told of a conversation between my grandson, Kai (who was six at the time) and his dad, Matt. Kai was walking home with his dad and his two-year-old brother, who was on Matt's shoulders, slumped over Matt's head, fast asleep. Matt was holding on to Martin's feet (trying to keep him securely on his shoulders) and Kai's hand. The three of them came to a busy street they needed to cross, but Matt was having difficulty getting a clear view of the road. So he asked Kai, "Do you see any cars coming?"

Kai replied, "Dad, you should say, 'Look both ways to see if any cars are coming.'"

"You're right, Kai. Look both ways. Do you see any cars coming?"

"Dad, you should say, 'Do you see any trucks coming too?'"

Just as Kai instinctively understood the value of clear questions, different types of questions help clarify the spiritual journey. Different types of questions present different ways to explore an individual's spiritual house.

Spiritual questions have at their core a desire for all to become more like Christ for the sake of others. Asking questions is a way to explore an individual's spiritual house. The following list of question types begins with easy ones (used for introductions and ends), with others used only when trust and rapport are fully established. When trust is established, then we can move through a person's inner house without making them feel afraid or ashamed.

Knocking on the Door

Beginning questions are usually easy to answer. Most people are not anxious or confused by them. They are not intimidated or worried about answering. These questions are a starting point for knowing the person and his or her spirituality. Beginning spiritual questions are not leading questions. Leading questions are asked when someone wants a particular answer. These questions, on the other hand, have no right answers. A person may respond in any manner they wish without any fear of judgment. These are great questions for the first time you meet as a Mentoring Community. Some examples include

- What is your earliest memory of a house you grew up in? What was it like? Where did you live?
- Who is the first person who helped you know God?
- What is your earliest experience of God?
- Who is your spiritual hero / role model?
- What is a story from your life that represents the essence of who you are?
- What is a story from your childhood that brings you joy?
- Where do you worship? What do you like best about your church?
- When you think of God, what Bible image or picture comes to mind?
- Which memory from your childhood brings you the most joy?

Entering the Main House

These are classic spiritual questions used throughout the ages. They go a little deeper and allow a person to express their spiritual desires. Also, these questions do not have any particular answer. People might respond in a variety of ways. They are open questions, so people can answer as deeply as they want, but the questions do begin to reveal something of the Holy Spirit's movement in the answerer.

These questions invite you into each other's inner lives in a polite, noninvasive way, as if you are respectful guests to each other. Once the Mentoring Community is going, these questions can help frame sharing and prayer times. They are an invitation to begin the journey. These classic questions help us understand the core spiritual desires for people in the Mentoring Community.

The following questions were crafted in the sixteenth century by a man named Ignatius.[3] They explore current movements within a person: toward God (consolations) or away from God (desolations). They are not sophisticated, but they help describe the current spiritual reality of a mentee or peer. These are open questions, so the sharer brings whatever level of intensity or investment he or she desires.

- What is your desire for God?
- What is God's desire for you?
- What are hindrances?

Entering the Kitchen

Once a person feels comfortable with a mentor and his or her peers, deeper questions can be asked. Trusted friends are invited into the interior spaces of one's inner house. The mentor and peers can invite the person to share more: How do they usually experience God, what are their specific feelings right now, and what have they done to nurture a relationship with God? At this point in the relationship, the mentor and peers begin exploring the spiritual house of an individual, becoming familiar with its habits, pitfalls, graces, and struggles.

- What is the story of your childhood, life, and spiritual journey? Include the history of your family and your growing-up experiences.

- When in your childhood did you feel the most sorrow?

- What are your predominate feelings about your relationship with God?

- Do you have any internal movements, such things to discern or questions about life, faith, or your identity and calling? Share them.

- Are there specific blocks or temptations in your spiritual life? What are they, and what are you doing to address them?

- What are your *authentic* habits for sustaining your relationship with God?

- Who are your friends and closest relationships, and how are they sustaining you in your spiritual walk?

- Are there people with whom you are in a personal struggle? How are you managing it, within yourself and with God?

- Do you feel stuck emotionally, spiritually, or professionally? If so, how?

- How are you developing spiritually in your ministry?

- Is your pace sustainable? Why or why not?

- Is your heart for God increasing or decreasing? Why?

- Is your heart for others increasing or decreasing? Why?

Bringing All the House's Rooms into God's Presence

Usually, when people share stories of their lives and spiritual journeys, one or two carry more emotion, distress, or energy than the others. These intense stories open up places in their lives that might have huge spiritual implications. The stories themselves can be as insignificant as a small boy breaking a rule or as huge as a car accident in which someone dies.

They are difficult to discern on our own effort, but with the input of the Holy Spirit, it is possible to hear something we might normally miss. I listen very carefully to the whole story, and I listen for the event that seems to bear more weight than others. It is a catalytic moment in that person's life. When I hear one, I often ask the mentee to tell me more about what happened. The catalytic moment might be an event of grace or one of darkness.

Once a mentee began by telling me she had never experienced God in her life. So, I asked her to tell me her life story. While telling the story, she briefly shared a strange experience she had as a small girl observing a flower in a meadow. When she finished telling her life story, I asked her to tell me more about that meadow experience. We spent ten minutes or more on a story she had previously mentioned in a few seconds. I kept asking her questions until it became real to her again, rather than a half-forgotten moment in her past. She had had a mystical experience of God's glory. As a little girl, she had understood that it was a personal revelation of God to her, but as an adult, this truth was buried in the present difficulties of her life. Rediscovering that story led her to recall other times when she experienced God through people and through God's unusual provision. She moved from believing that God didn't care about her to a sense of God's watching over her throughout her life.

These are invitation types of questions. The peers or mentor bring to life something tucked away and forgotten. When we ask such questions, we are looking for a way to let in light or let out darkness. Sometimes, this type of focused questioning on an event can lead to a healing prayer or profound awareness.

Can we go back to _____? Tell me more about it. What do you see? What do you smell? What are you feeling? Where are you standing? Are you alone? What's going through your mind? Is anyone else there?

Well-asked questions are invitations into the authentic realities—spiritual, emotional, relational, and professional—of people in the Mentoring Community. These questions can lead to deeper insights. If we are to love each other, then we need to know each other. If we are to encourage each other, we need to understand each other's struggles. If we are to hold each other in the dark, we need to know the temptations and challenges. These often don't come without thoughtful, Spirit-guided questions. In Mentoring Communities, we linger together with the Holy Spirit for insight, healing, and transformation.

We grow in trust of one another, and collectively we keep step with God more consistently as we open ourselves to each other's probing questions and as we learn to ask penetrating questions that reflect each other's status as Christ followers. So, what is the etiquette for asking spiritual questions in Mentoring Communities?

Manners for Asking Spiritual Questions

Having good manners at home is a way to show respect. I always had my children wait to serve themselves and eat until everyone, including the cook, was seated at the table. I wanted my children to respect the time and effort it took to prepare a meal for them. In spiritual conversations, good manners are simply the way of honoring someone by treating everyone in the community with respect and care. Here are a few guidelines for good manners when asking spiritual questions.

1. Ask questions that focus on the person sharing, not on you. When another person has the floor, resist the temptation to share stories about yourself, give explanations about your views, experiences, or theology, or ask questions that lead back to you.

2. Keep the questions open, not closed. Questions that get a "yes" or "no" answer or lead the person sharing to a specific conclusion are closed. Open questions give people opportunities to honestly share whatever is going on within them.

3. Always ask permission to go deeper. "Do you mind if I go a little deeper?" "May I ask you a follow-up question?" "May I push back on that a little bit?" None of the above types of questions can be forced.

4. It's a stroll, not a sprint. Match the pace of the person's emotional state and stamina. If the person is depressed, tired, or anxious, requesting that they share more is not helpful.

Asking spiritual questions in mentoring relationships honors the person we are hosting. It says that we want to know more, that we care. That we believe everyone has a rich, beautiful spiritual world to explore. It says that darkness isn't the end and light can always be found. It says that we are listening, and we will go with them wherever the Holy Spirit leads. It is the role of the mentor and Mentoring Community to notice the duck, to notice what might be missed without our careful attentiveness and gentle questions.

In Mentoring Communities, there are three ways spiritual questions might be used. First, as the group gets to know each other, it's very helpful to build trust by first knocking on the door, then entering the house, and then—after the previous questions—exploring the rest of the house. Going into the interior of one's inner house without first building trust and getting to know each other well usually results in someone hiding their true self. Trust is earned when trust is built, so asking spiritual questions from the beginning builds the foundation to press into intimate questions that allow us to see each other's true self and authentic walk with God.

When I begin a group or train people to start groups, I go through the question exercises that always start with the knocking-on-the-door questions that lead into the kitchen. When people experience the wonder of being asked questions and then truly listened to, they yearn for more of the companionship of a Mentoring Community.

Second, when the group is practicing the core discipline of Group Listening Prayer (which is covered in chapter 10), sometimes after a person has shared, someone in the group might want to ask for more understanding into something the person shared. Generally, questions are not asked at this time, except for clarification.

In my group, a member recently shared about challenging events in his workplace and how he was discerning his next move. After he finished sharing, another member of the group asked a question: "Last time we were together, you shared how you experienced God in your artwork, but you didn't mention it this time. What is happening with your art and your experience of God as you paint?" Because of the trust already built, it was the right question to ask. The sharer went on to reveal much more of his walk with God and his inner state by showing photos of his recent work.

A third way spiritual questions might be used is during the informal times when the group is on retreat together. Often, the mentor meets with each person individually, so the questions are a way to get to know each person better or follow up with them. The group often eats together, so mealtimes are great times to ask these types of questions. If the group is on a walk or out doing something else together, it is always an opportunity to bring the focus to Christ and each other's journey toward wholeness for God's glory.

> *Have patience with everything unresolved in your heart*
> *and . . . try to love the questions themselves. . . .*
> *Don't search for the answers,*
> *which could not be given to you now,*
> *because you would not be able to live them.*
> *And the point is to live everything.*
> *Live the questions now.*
> *Perhaps then, someday far in the future,*
> *you will gradually, without even noticing it,*
> *live your way into the answer.*
>
> RAINER MARIA RILKE, *Letters to a Young Poet*[4]

Discernment

When we learn to hear God's voice,
we find our own true voice.

LEIGHTON FORD

A MEMBER OF A MENTORING COMMUNITY shared this story with me and gave me permission to include it here. I'm going to refer to him as Dave. Dave's group was meeting for its sixth time, and he couldn't wait until they gathered because he felt very stuck. He had a complicated discernment problem about next steps in his calling. Over the past year, since the group had last met, Dave had been unable to discern what he should do next. He was serving full-time as the discipleship pastor in a thriving church. Because of his success, he also had a fruitful ministry teaching and training, nationally and internationally. What had been ten years of satisfying ministry became one long year of frustration and confusion when a new senior pastor began undermining Dave's programs. The new pastor did not believe in the discipleship model Dave had developed with a committed team of lay leaders. The senior pastor was convinced that they should use the model of a well-known megachurch.

Dave didn't have any problems with the megachurch model, but he and his lay team knew it wouldn't work very well in their context. The model Dave and his team developed was tailored for the demographics, culture, needs, and theology of their church. But the new senior pastor was not interested in Dave's perspective. Dave was torn about what to do next. Should he move on to another ministry? The pastor didn't want Dave to leave. He recognized that Dave was a hard worker, and the pastor knew he could rely on him to do his job well. Dave also had a son and daughter in high school, and his wife loved her social-work job at the local hospital. He loved the people in the congregation, and his wife's parents, who lived nearby, were not in good health and depended on them for care and support.

On the second morning of the gathering, Dave felt ready to share. After the opening silence, he told the story of what had transpired since they had last met. He was hurt watching his ministry come apart. He was conflicted about whether to stay or move on. He took his time telling the story. After he shared his story, the group entered the silence again. Then, one by one, the group shared; the theme was the same, although everyone's words were different. One member summed it up by saying, "I saw this teacup, and the Lord said, 'Your call is bigger than the teacup. Throw the cup into the sea and trust God's call.'"

Dave knew immediately that the group had discerned rightly for him. He felt the Holy Spirit pierce his heart with the truth. God's call was not to a place but to a people. He felt unburdened and was ready to move to wherever God called him and his family.

Hearing God's Voice and Discernment

In describing Mentoring Communities, Leighton Ford wrote, "Spiritual mentoring/direction is not a program, or a technique, or a profession. It is an art: the art of listening to and with others in the presence of Another. . . . A central mark of our community will be a commitment to help each other to listen: to God, to our own hearts, and to each other."[1]

A central part of the maturing-in-Christ process is becoming increasingly familiar with the presence and voice of God. Before coming to faith, we walked our own paths, but after coming to faith, we want to walk God's path. Mentoring Communities provide a safe place and safe people for discerning God's voice and presence in decisions big and small.

Ordinary Discernment is hearing God in the everyday. It requires times for solitude and silence and reflection with others. Two spiritual disciplines for Ordinary Discernment are the Examen and Lectio Divina, or Reflective Bible Reading. The Examen gives space for reflecting on God's presence in the ordinary day and allows us to discern patterns in our lives. Reflective Bible Reading and Scripture Memorization allow God to speak to us throughout the day.

Extraordinary Discernment is hearing God in life's big questions and decision points, and it requires community and accountability. Mentoring Communities and group-discernment practices offer prayer, wisdom, prophetic insight, and companionship, which is critical for discerning major questions.

Personal and Community Discernment— Five Paths to God's Way

Five paths lead to Ordinary and Extraordinary Discernment. These are Scripture, the Holy Spirit, Stillness and Quiet, Submission and Trust, and Listening in Community.

Scripture

Indeed, the word of God is living and active, sharper than any two-edged sword, piercing until it divides soul from spirit, joints from marrow; it is able to judge the thoughts and intentions of the heart.

HEBREWS 4:12

All scripture is inspired by God and is useful for teaching, for reproof, for correction, and for training in righteousness, so that everyone who belongs to God may be proficient, equipped for every good work.

2 TIMOTHY 3:16-17

The written Word of God is a primary resource for knowing and understanding the character and will of God. Through Scripture Jesus, God's only Son, is revealed, and we understand our primary calling to be the people of God's Kingdom. If something is clearly contrary to God's Word, then it is not of God.

Sometimes our understanding of God's Word is not so clear. In our finiteness and fallenness, we can err in our interpretation. We are nurtured in a particular faith context and church and in a particular cultural context, which can limit our understanding. So, sometimes we discover a fresh understanding of God's heart and mind.

For instance, slavery was common at one point in history, and it was supported by the church's interpretation of Scripture. Now we understand the arc of Scripture differently. Nowhere would the Christian church support slavery today. Because of our limitations, therefore, we need other avenues for knowing the will of God. From Scripture, we learn that the Holy Spirit is given to us precisely to help us know and understand God's truth.

The Holy Spirit

[Jesus said,] "And I will ask the Father, and he will give you another Advocate, to be with you forever. This is the Spirit of truth, whom the world cannot receive, because it neither sees him nor knows him. You know him, because he abides with you, and he will be in you."

JOHN 14:16-17

[Jesus said,] "But the Advocate, the Holy Spirit, whom the Father will send in my name, will teach you everything, and remind you of all that I have said to you."

JOHN 14:26

The Holy Spirit reveals to us God's nature and God's will for us. The Holy Spirit knows us intimately and knows our true identity in Christ.

The Holy Spirit is often able to connect our passions and desires with opportunities. But sometimes we forget that the Spirit is given precisely as a Helper to guide us in truth. We need to learn to cultivate the presence of the Holy Spirit. With our busy lives, we often neglect to pay attention to the Holy Spirit in ordinary days. We miss the Holy Spirit's revelations and guiding presence. We also need Stillness and Quiet to create space to pay attention to the Spirit.

Stillness and Quiet

> Be still, and know that I am God!
> > I am exalted among the nations,
> > I am exalted in the earth.

PSALM 46:10

> [Jesus said,] "Peace I leave with you; my peace I give to you. I do not give to you as the world gives. Do not let your hearts be troubled, and do not let them be afraid."

JOHN 14:27

In order to discern the meaning of Scripture through the Holy Spirit, we have to create space in our lives for Stillness and Quiet. We have to remove all the noise in our heads and to lay aside the demands on our lives. Busyness needs to cease for the calling of the Spirit to come clear. In prayer and Reflective Bible Study, we create space for the Stillness and Quiet precisely so the Holy Spirit might flourish in us. The space created is not just to take a rest from life's demands but to listen and to discern the way of God. With the Holy Spirit, we need to take time to observe.

This observing is both within and outside our own souls. We quiet ourselves and listen to what is stirring within us and what is happening around us. What leads you away from God, or what makes you depressed or sad or guilty? How might you develop trust in God? Notice your feelings and emotions and how they might be informing you. Listen for the still, small voice of God. This listening requires silence and solitude, quieting all the noise and busyness of your life. Discernment does not come just from fervent prayer but from a life of listening. But stillness without Submission and Trust is not very helpful.

Submission and Trust

I appeal to you therefore, brothers and sisters, by the mercies of God, to present your bodies as a living sacrifice, holy and acceptable to God, which is your spiritual worship. Do not be conformed to this world, but be transformed by the renewing of your minds, so that you may discern what is the will of God—what is good and acceptable and perfect.

ROMANS 12:1-2

But I am like a green olive tree
    in the house of God.
I trust in the steadfast love of God
    forever and ever.

PSALM 52:8

Let me hear of your steadfast love in the morning,
    for in you I put my trust.
Teach me the way I should go,
    for to you I lift up my soul.

PSALM 143:8

With Scripture and the Holy Spirit, and in Stillness and Quiet, discernment is most likely if we are completely submitted to God and we trust God's goodness and mercy. If we have doubts or are fearful, angry, or depressed, it is difficult to hear God's voice. Our voices of pain can crowd out the presence of the Spirit. This is very human. Instead of fighting to discern what we should do, we are being called to enter our suffering. As we come to understand our distress, what it really means, we can trust God for the reality of God in the midst of suffering. This is usually very difficult to accomplish without others. We need others to pray for us and help us trust our God.

Listening in Community

> By the grace given to me I say to everyone among you not to think of yourself more highly than you ought to think, but to think with sober judgment, each according to the measure of faith that God has assigned. For as in one body we have many members, and not all the members have the same function, so we, who are many, are one body in Christ, and individually we are members one of another.
>
> ROMANS 12:3-5

> They devoted themselves to the apostles' teaching and *fellowship*, to the breaking of bread and the prayers.
>
> ACTS 2:42, EMPHASIS ADDED

> If we walk in the light as he himself is in the light, we have *fellowship* with one another, and the blood of Jesus his Son cleanses us from all sin.
>
> I JOHN 1:7, EMPHASIS ADDED

God created us to be in community. We are known best when we are a family committed to one another for the long haul. In Mentoring Communities, we learn to know and love each other well, and we are particularly called together to discern the health of our walk with God, the strength of our primary relationships, and the directions of our ministries.

Of course, we also have pastors, counselors, coaches, parents, and elders to support our individual journeys. But Mentoring Community members have no agenda for each other besides fully thriving in Christ, so they are a safe place and a balance to other voices. This does not mean that Mentoring Communities always get it right. Mentoring

Communities are a unique way to provide safety, prayer, and account-ability in a loving environment for all members.

Mentoring Communities create environments for practicing all five aspects of discernment. The communities use Scripture, listen to the Holy Spirit, create times for Stillness and Quiet, Submit and Trust together, and Listen in Community.

Discernment Definition and Process

Nick Valadez shares the following about what is meant by discernment *and how discernment works in practice.*

On a late September afternoon in 2011, I was walking home from the office where I work as a therapist. It was a crisp fall day, and by the end of the walk, I could hardly wait to see my wife, Mindi. I had something very important to share with her. For the first time in months, I felt free! After eight months of relative confusion, clarity came on that five-minute walk home. A very important decision about our future had come to me as I walked.

Since graduating from seminary, I had been working at three part-time jobs. I was the administrative assistant and Mentoring Community coordinator for Dr. Leighton Ford and Leighton Ford Ministries. I was also working at a private psychology practice, counseling caregivers, leaders, and their families. My third position was as the associate direc-tor of counseling programs at Gordon–Conwell Theological Seminary in Charlotte, North Carolina.

I had a passion for the people and relationships within each of these places, but I simply could not give full attention to any one of them while working part-time in all three. I felt torn between three seemingly equal possibilities. Was I to stay in an administrative support role with Leighton Ford Ministries' Mentoring Community? Should I be in an academic setting, helping ministry leaders train, grow, and thrive while in seminary? Could I settle into a full-time counseling rhythm, so I didn't burn out? I needed one full-time job, but which one should I pursue?

It was a tiring season of life that I knew I could not sustain for the long haul. I had to let go of something.

So I entered a steady rhythm of discernment through daily observations, listening, wrestling with feelings in solitude, time with my mentor and my Mentoring Community of friends, and the companionship of the Holy Spirit and Scripture. Little by little, I came to sense the Lord speaking to me with fullness and simplicity.

On that crisp September afternoon, while walking home, I heard the Spirit softly say, *I love you, I'm with you, and I will be with you no matter what.*

It was as if God confirmed what my parents had always modeled for me: that I could not make a wrong choice because I had their enduring love and support. No matter what I decided, Jesus was with me and would make things unfold for his purposes. It was an enlivening moment, full of peace and grace.

What I learned during those eight months of making a major decision also helps me in making smaller decisions of everyday life. I had learned to slow down, to pay attention to my own soul, to listen to my community, and most of all, to listen deeply for the voice of the Good Shepherd and touch of the Holy Spirit.

Discernment Defined

Discernment is sensing God's presence and finding the path of life. The goal is to listen deeply below the noise of ordinary life, to hear the Father's voice and direction, and to feel the impulses of love that draw us to our life's calling and shared mission. It requires trust to pause, wait, and reflect and courage to feel deeply, step out, and take action.

Discernment is not some vague, mystical path. The psalmist wrote, "I will instruct you and teach you the way you should go; I will counsel you with my eye upon you. Do not be like a horse or a mule, without understanding, whose temper must be curbed with bit and bridle" (Psalm 32:8-9). The Holy Spirit guides us through each part of ourselves. This is not strictly an intellectual pursuit or purely an emotional decision. It is both and more. Nor is it a matter of making lists of pros and cons, nor simply intuitional gut reactions. It is not a purely selfish or communal choice. It is inclusive, integrated, and whole, and it requires noticing each aspect of life. It is the spiritual practice of seeking awareness of what God is trying to communicate.

Discernment is learning to know and walk with God. Jesus says he is the Good Shepherd and the sheep know his voice. It takes spending time with a person (or shepherd) to really recognize their voice—their unique timbre, pitch, and pacing. It may take even more time and attentiveness to learn to recognize the nudges and whispers, the callings and graces of the Almighty.

Discernment must begin with intention, a clear heart desire to know and follow God. Then it takes great attention, closely attending to our own souls and to the heart of God. We can approach a season of discernment with eagerness and expectation, for in Deuteronomy, we read, "Surely, this commandment that I am commanding you today is not too hard for you, nor is it too far away. . . . No, the word is very near to you; it is in your mouth and in your heart for you to observe" (Deuteronomy 30:11, 14). Later, we read, "I have set before you life and death, blessings and curses. Choose life so that you and your descendants may live, loving the LORD your God, obeying him, and holding fast to him" (Deuteronomy 30:19-20).

The goal of discerning God's call is learning to choose life—step by step, day by day.

Discernment is different from problem-solving, where we are just looking for the answer to a question that seems to press in on us. This seems like a very simple and obvious thing to do to move forward. Why wouldn't we want the answer to our question? We have a question and we want an answer, period. But the answer is controlled by the question we ask. What if we have the wrong question? What if it is close but not quite the real question? If we have the wrong question, then the answer, if not wrong, will only be partial at best. What if there were a way to locate the real question, the underlying question, the leveraging question that reveals more than the answer—the pathway? That is discernment. Distinguishing the clear road from the good one and the deep question from the surface one is discernment.

Discernment is not just about direction but also about relationship. Our steps are ordered in the ways of the great command to love God and love our neighbors. By its very nature, discernment aims for a range of possibilities beyond the self. It may include the self and it may include the wisdom of community and others, but it primarily opens us up to God's way.

Purpose of Discernment

From the great Shema (Deuteronomy 6:4-9)[2] to the greatest commandments (Matthew 22:36-40), we are all called to give witness to the one true, sovereign God and to love him with our whole being. We are to do this each with our own uniqueness while united in oneness in him (John 17). Your distinctive presence in your family, neighborhood, and ministry is the way God desires you to be present to others and the world. Diverse people have diverse ways of being present. You must be familiar with and maintain your own unique, God-given way. That is why discernment is so essential. Once you have insight and awareness of your true calling, you have a point of reference and a course of action. This assists you in discerning what to do and what to release, when to stay home and when to go out, whom to be with and from whom to distance yourself, what to speak and what to hold silent. Discernment is internal and external attentiveness, examining daily signs and acknowledging messages from God.

When you get stressed, anxious, frustrated, exhausted, overwhelmed, or burned-out, your body may be telling you that the things you are doing are beyond your boundaries. God does not call you to do things outside your capacity and ability. He wants you to live for others and to live that presence well. Doing so might include suffering, fatigue, and even moments of great physical or emotional pain, but none of this must ever pull you away from your deepest self (your identity) and your life in God.

Sometimes it is difficult to find your place in your community. Your way of being present to your neighbors may require times of absence, prayer, writing, or solitude. These, too, are times for your community. Times of discernment allow you to be deeply attuned to your people and speak words that come from God through you. When it is part of your calling to offer people insight and foresight that will nurture them and allow them to keep moving forward, it is critical that you give yourself the time and space to let that vision develop in you and become an integral part of your being.

It is worth noting that we often fail to see the things we don't expect. For this reason, we must move beyond our natural abilities and wisdom and open ourselves completely to God and what he might reveal to us. In this way, wonder is an aspect of discernment, a way of openness to the unexpected.

Times for Discernment

Typically, we think of discernment when we have a big decision to make, like my decision about job direction. And certainly, all of us face key turning points in our lives that require careful discernment: what to study, where to work, whom to marry, where to live. These might be called *acts* of discernment, which require disciplines and careful direction-seeking over time.

Perhaps more important is cultivating the ongoing *habit* of discernment. This is discerning God's voice in the everyday: calling to reach out to a friend, taking time to read a certain passage of Scripture, hurrying home to find a family member in need, or taking the walkway to the right, which turns out to have a beautiful flower blooming for your praise. Leighton's book *The Attentive Life* speaks about cultivating this way of being alert and present to God throughout our days.[3] A good friend reminds me that life rarely presents big decisions if one has been faithfully discerning the small steps all along life's path.

Discernment is a personal and a communal process. We have Scriptures and the Holy Spirit to guide us. We create space for Stillness and Listening, both by ourselves and in community. We have conversations and pray in our Mentoring Communities, and we Submit and Trust in how God reveals to us the way through all the avenues of guidance. Personal discernment and group discernment work together. Group discernment is especially helpful in getting us to bear witness—out loud—to our current situation or questions. Group discernment also holds us accountable to act on the Spirit's leading. One form of stuckness is to be always discerning but never responding to a way forward.

Group discernment doesn't absolve us from individual work. It is not one or the other; it is both. If we rely only on individual discernment, it can become a kind of self-protective fortress preventing other people from speaking into our lives. If we rely only on the group, we don't take responsibility for what God is doing uniquely in us. Jesus did not discern with the disciples whether he should go to the cross. We need to protect and nourish the precious development of our identity and mission in Christ and for Christ.

Group Listening Prayer

The Core Spiritual Discipline of Mentoring Communities

Written by Anne Grizzle

Nowhere else have I encountered an environment so structured to grow, support, and facilitate ministry. I am young, naive, and often foolish, but knowing I have a group to help reflect and discuss the happenings of ministry gives me great hope for the coming years.

MICHAEL, MINISTRY TRAINEE (AUSTRALIA)

DURING A RETREAT I WAS OFFERING, I volunteered to host a session of Group Listening Prayer Saturday afternoon for anyone who wished to come. Five participants and I began with ten minutes of silence, then I offered each person present the opportunity to share something on their heart for which they would like the group to listen to God. The first woman shared, after which we returned to silence to listen to God. After a few minutes, I rang a bell and invited anyone to share if a simple image or word had come as they prayed. We continued around the circle until each woman had shared and the group had listened and then briefly responded. As we were about to end, one of the women asked if they could listen for me. "Sure," I said, "I never pass on prayer." I shared that our family was moving to DC, and I wanted to be open to whatever God had for me in this new move. We went into silent listening. After several minutes, I gave an opportunity for sharing. One woman looked a bit quizzical and said, "I had this image of a green hill and sheep grazing." Another somewhat apologetically said, "I got something sort of funny. Not sure if I should share it—it's a line from an old movie." I said, "We simply offer what comes, so feel free to share." She then gave the line "If you build it, they will come." I was astounded at the gift from these novices in this prayer practice to me. Unbeknownst to them, I was in the process of building a home for retreats that was a hard project to complete. It was on land with a green hill where I wanted to invite other sheep of God's fold to come for refreshment. These words from listening, praying strangers were a great confirmation and encouragement in the season ahead!

Much of the prayer I have heard in groups contains many, many words from people and almost no room for hearing from God. Certainly, we need to pour out our souls before God, and in groups, we also want to intercede for one another with heartfelt words. But for our relationships with God and others to grow deeper, lots of listening is critical. Listening Prayer is a way to make room for listening not only to our souls and one another but also to God in the middle of our gathering.[1] As a loving community in Christ listens for one another, the Holy Spirit shows up in remarkable ways with grace and guidance.

We have found in our Mentoring Communities that a simple process helps us go more deeply in listening prayerfully together. We come trusting the promise of Jesus: "Where two or three are gathered in my name, I am there among them" (Matthew 18:20). I first learned this at a spiritual-guidance program, from Rose Mary Dougherty, who wrote *Group Spiritual Direction: Community for Discernment*, which outlines this process in greater detail.[2] I have taught this process to groups young and old, in churches and communities, for many years. As taught by Rose Mary Dougherty, four people gather prayerfully over the course of two hours. But this process of listening and sharing is possible with different sizes of groups and for different amounts of time. Group Listening Prayer is an important core practice of Mentoring Communities.

Setting

Group Listening Prayer works best when participants are in an environment where they will not be disturbed. If people are walking by or chatting, it is difficult to maintain the focus necessary for listening to each other and the Holy Spirit. A location should be chosen that allows for optimum quiet, without the possibility of disruption. My group met in a living-room area one year. We were in our usual circle, and we had opened the sliding door for fresh air. After we began and were deep in prayer for the first person, a grounds keeper began mowing the lawn. We laughed and shut the door. Being in a restful, quiet place helps everyone to bring his or her best self to the listening experience.

Another helpful logistic is to have participants in a circle so everyone can see each other's faces and hear each other's voices. This assures every group member that this is a safe place and these are safe people and helps diminish the temptation to look at watches or phones. Attentiveness is the foremost sign of affection. Facing each other makes that impression clear.

Some groups like to put a small table in the center with a candle, cross, open Bible, or some spiritual artwork on top. By lighting a candle, we remind ourselves that Christ is the Light of the World and is with us. I like to have a Bible opened to a passage that has significance for the group—perhaps a passage that's come up earlier in the retreat setting. Some groups include artists and lovers of God's beautiful world and like to place symbols and representations on the little table. These things are not necessary, but they set a table of hospitality for listening.

One person, usually the mentor or a peer chosen for the role, leads the process. That person pays attention to time during silences and listening parts. Everyone can relax as one person takes responsibility for hosting the sharing-and-listening time. In order to signal the end of silence, the facilitator can ring a little bell or set a timer on a smartphone. A simple "Amen" also works. Now that the setting is arranged, the process is as follows.

Steps in Group Listening Prayer

Step one—prayer of silence: Listening Prayer uses silence as a way of consciously making space for God. Silence is less about not talking and more about having a posture of open, attentive listening for God. Group Listening Prayer typically begins with a longer period of silence. This might be ten to fifteen minutes. If the group is already in a quiet retreat frame of mind, the opening silence might be for only ten minutes. The mentor or chosen peer facilitator may light the candle and say, "Be still and know that I am God" or offer another Scripture as a way of leading the group into silence, if they wish. The silence gives everyone time to still the inner chatter in their minds and turn their loving attention to God by gazing on him and receiving his loving gaze. In that inner place of love, group members also have time to listen to their own souls to discern what the Spirit might be stirring that they want the group to consider in prayer.

Step two—first sharing: After the initial silence, one member begins sharing what they want the group to consider. In Mentoring Communities, usually an hour is set aside for each person. Half of the time is for the person to share whatever they have on their heart to share. Usually, there is a review of what happened since the last time the group met and then a reflection on what is needed for discernment and prayer now. If the group is meeting for the first time, it is important for the person sharing to tell their spiritual story (to acquaint the group with their life and ministry), then reveal their core concern.

Remarkably, the sharing and prayer requests that come after a period of silence are different from what comes when we ask for prayer requests without that space for listening. Without centering silence, many of us lack easy access to the deeper needs of our souls, so we are

> *In Group Listening Prayer, in between the sharing and the response, I was very touched by five minutes of silence. You really feel like the Holy Spirit is speaking to you.*
>
> EMMANUEL (KENYA)

more inclined to share pressing-but-less-significant concerns: "My dad is dying—pray for my dad" rather than "My dad is dying, and my mom is pushing all my buttons." What God is working in our souls is often different from what is happening externally in our lives. This is what we want to hear from one another. This is what we want to lift up to God for one another.

Sharing in Listening Prayer does not require lots of details. Whatever helps to convey the essence of the sharer's heart concern is needed, but not all the details surrounding it. Listeners can ask a clarifying question but only if it helps bring understanding. If some part of the sharing was confusing, a group member might ask for clarification. After all, we will be lifting this person to God, and God knows everything, so we don't need every bit of information.

Every person in the group who is not sharing at this point is a listener and a person of prayer. The whole time of listening to someone, while they are talking and during silence, is with an attitude of attentiveness to the Spirit. As we listen to a person sharing, we have one ear to the person and the other ear to God. The only person talking is the person sharing.

Step three—listening silence on behalf of the person who shared: After a person has shared, the entire group returns to silence. The mentor or facilitator might say, "Let us return to silence to lift this person into the light and love of God and listen for God's prayer for them." This silence usually lasts five to eight minutes. Listeners are like the friends of the paralytic that we read about in Mark 2:1-12. They let their friend down before Jesus. In silence, the person who shared is lifted into God's light. Listening starts from the assumption that God knows and loves this person completely, so we do not need to tell God what he already knows. Listening also starts with the assumption that Jesus is at the right hand of God, interceding for the one who shared (Romans 8:34). The group seeks to join in the prayer of Jesus for this person. In the silence, listeners are not telling God what they think the one who shared needs; rather, they are attentively listening for a sense of what God's prayer might be for this person. Just having a few friends lovingly hold an individual before God is gift enough.

Step four—response to the person who shared: The facilitator breaks the silence with a bell or by saying "Amen." After silence for listening, those who have been listening are invited to share anything that they experienced. Sometimes in the listening, a Scripture, image, or song might arise. It is also common for the mind to wander from this person's sharing to our own, similar experiences, or to begin concocting advice for the person, or even to reflect on passages of Scripture that their story evoked for you. Acknowledge and moved on from these wanderings. They are to be distinguished from the word or image or Scripture that the Lord might bring to your mind for this person. We hold these things before God during this time of silence to see if they continue to resonate.

Those who share their listening experiences must let go of things they feel are just their own best idea or response and use this time only to share what seems to come from prayerfulness. In addition, this is not the time to extend the sharing by telling stories or having the one who shared say more. The listeners should be sharing, not the talker. A simple offering of an image, word, or prayer that has come is sufficient. It is very helpful when someone offers to take notes on what is shared on behalf of the one who shared. This allows the sharer to listen fully to the one speaking but also preserves what was spoken.

In addition, there is no need for the offerings to necessarily make clear sense. The "if you build it, they will come" line given to me after silence made sense to me, even though it didn't to the person who shared it! Also, offer what comes without a sense of a strong prophetic voice but rather as a humble, gentle offering. Allow the sharer to discern what resonates with the Spirit for them. This is listening for only a few minutes by a gathered community of humble believers. We offer our love and prayers in love. Sometimes something resonates profoundly. Other times, the surrounding love of prayerfulness is gift enough. What is key is that we have listened attentively and deeply to one another with a prayerfulness to God.

Step five—prayer for the person who shared: After hearing the responses, the person who shared can offer any final comments, if they wish. Then the mentor or peer facilitator asks who would like to pray for the one who shared. Someone volunteers to pray. It is helpful to lay hands on the one who shared while praying aloud as a way of expressing the group's love and involvement in the prayer. The brief spoken prayer places the needs and responses in God's care.

Step six—return to silence: At the end of the prayer, it might be helpful to see if anyone needs a short break. If two or three people will be listened to in the span of a determined amount of time, it is helpful to take a little break to stretch, get a drink, or use the facilities. This should only be five minutes. If a break is not needed, the group returns to a short silence, out of which the next person can share.

Step seven—repeat the process: The process of one person sharing, group silent Listening Prayer, offering responses, and final prayer continues until everyone in the group has had an opportunity to share and have prayer with the group. At the end, it's helpful to take a few minutes to reflect on the group's prayerfulness as a group. This can help an ongoing group learn as they go and note any concerns or ways they might need to grow. The facilitator can bring the time to conclusion with a collectively spoken Lord's Prayer or a simple prayer or benediction.

Holding the Space

The process of group listening is simple yet results in profound connecting in prayerful community. It's important for the mentor or another person experienced in the process to take responsibility for holding the space, for leading the group into silence, for inviting responses, for bringing the group back to focus if it gets off track, and

> *Spiritually, Group Listening Prayer was very intense and draining. Immersion and reflection take energy. I felt drained, but I really believe as a result of this day that amazing things will happen in different places. I thank God for being part of this. It's a revolution in practicing the presence of Christ, being with Christ.*
>
> BABU (KENYA)

for keeping the time, so everyone has opportunity to share and have prayerful listening.

Several challenges often arise in learning this process. First, it can be easy to move out of prayerfulness. When someone offers a response, they can go on too long. Others might jump in with their own responses to the response. Cross talk can happen, and prayerfulness is lost. The process requires *holding a continuing sense of attentiveness to God*, a sense that we are in holy space and speak not from a chatty place but rather a heart space, with only as many words as necessary to convey the heart.

While all members of the group are responsible for keeping this prayerfulness, the facilitator has a particular responsibility to set the tone and then gently return the group to prayerfulness with a comment such as "Let's return to some quiet" or "Let's hold discussion and allow _____ to ponder what has been offered out of our prayerfulness."

Another challenge is when participants think they need to have a profound, godly response. Sometimes we simply hold another person in prayerful love. Great visions do not come; yet a simple offering of "I sensed rays of light in your direction" or "My heart was hurting with your pain, which I held before God" is fine. Sometimes a blessed image comes, and the person feels embarrassed to offer it because it does not seem to be beautiful or make sense. This requires a willingness of all to simply offer what comes with the understanding the recipient can do as they wish with the offering. Other times, participants may have visions so robust and regular or voiced with such a sense of authority from God that it can be a bit overwhelming. The group's prayerful presence does not guarantee that everything spoken comes directly from God; it simply gives expression to willingness to be present to God for one another. Remembering to stay humble and simple in our prayerfulness gives this process its gentle power. Keeping the wisdom from the book of James helps ground this process: "Let everyone be quick to listen, slow to speak" (James 1:19).

Finally, sometimes we are challenged when someone shares deep confusion or pain, and we want to make everything right. We want to make the person feel better or solve their problem. In her book, Rose Mary says, "At times the strength of spiritual community lies in the love of people who refrain from getting caught in the trap of trying to fix everything for us, who pray for us and allow us the pain of our wilderness, our wants, so that we might become more deeply grounded in God."[3] Willingness to be a friend of Job—without unnecessary words, yet able to sit with the pain in love—is the powerful work of being a compassionate witness, which is a witness to passionately staying with Job in love.

A great benefit of this way of praying is how it develops community. All members share and listen prayerfully for each other, so the process builds a great sense of communion in Christ. We discover the truth of that African proverb that the reason two antelopes walk together is so one can blow the dust from the other's eyes.

For me, the experience of Group Listening Prayer was refreshing. It was really refreshing to have an opportunity to share in an environment with your friends. The concept is relevant in any culture. Safe people, safe places is based on trust and confidence. These people have good intentions for you and are there for you.

JOHN (RWANDA)

This process is particularly powerful when used in its full form and on an ongoing basis with a group, but the idea of using silence for listening to God rather than responding with immediate reactions can be used in all kinds of mentoring relationships. In my mentor groups, the heart of our days allows time for each member to share with the group from their life the past year. After the person finishes, we have time for a few clarifying questions. But then we stop for silence to pray for the person and listen to God. Afterward, our comments come from that prayerful listening space. When we only share in this way and do not take time for corresponding Listening Prayer, members feel that lack of going to the next level of sharing. What Listening Prayer offers is a place where we go beneath the surface—beyond what we might think we ought to share to other rivers of the Spirit in our souls. And we share in a context where we know movemenets of the Spirit will be held in precious prayer. The wonders of communion with God and one another seem particularly rich when we listen in this way together.

Simple Outline of Group Listening Prayer Format

Prayer of silence: The facilitator opens with a short prayer acknowledging the love and presence of God, then the group is prayerfully silent for ten to fifteen minutes. Each group member takes this time to set aside distractions and listen deeply to God and for what is stirring within their soul that they wish to share for prayerfulness with the group.

First sharing: Out of the silence, whoever feels led begins by sharing from their spiritual journey whatever callings, concerns, struggles, and reflections they wish for thirty minutes. The content shared should be from the sharer's current, ongoing relationship with God, with a desire for prayer and support.

- The rest of the group listens prayerfully without comment or question.
- The group holds the person before God in their hearts as they share.
- Only simple, clarifying questions may be asked, at the end.

Listening silence on behalf of the person who shared: When the first person finishes sharing, return to Listening Prayer and silence for five to eight minutes. Lift the person into God's light and love with the gentle question, *Lord, what is your prayer for this person?* Beware of any desire to coach, counsel, admonish, or share personal stories. Set these thoughts aside and listen deeply for the Holy Spirit.

Response to the person who shared: After three to five minutes, the facilitator invites the group to ask the person who shared a question, make a comment, or bring a word from God.

Prayer for the person who shared: When everyone who desires to respond has finished, one person volunteers to pray a simple prayer of blessing and encouragement for the one who shared.

Return to silence: Return to a few minutes of silence, out of which the next person may share.

Repeat the process: Repeat the process until all have shared.

If your group meets more regularly than once a year, you can adapt the Group Listening Prayer to include group-discernment questions (see chapter 9).

PART THREE

The Mentoring Community Experience

11

The Rhythm of Spiritual
Mentoring Communities

*Like many pastors focused on making sure everyone else is taken care of, I
was not accustomed to peers who were willing to sit and listen to God just
for me, and I needed it desperately. My group's care has made God seem more
attentive. Each year, I look forward to this week when we freshen friendships,
hear God for each other, pray together, eat good food, tell each other our
stories, rest in the presence of great natural beauty, and enjoy God's presence.*

D. LOYD, PASTOR (USA)

GOD CREATED US FOR REST and activity, and Jesus commanded us
to "go . . . and make disciples" and to abide in him. Without ongoing
connection to the Vine, there can be no fruit. We also know that God
created us to be in community, to belong and to be known as individuals. Adam needed a companion, but Adam and Eve were separate individuals. We are in a worldwide family of believers, yet we are individuals
fulfilling God's call on our lives.

The sign that we are the people of God, that we are redeemed and set
apart for God's favor and purpose, is that we love each other. These are
clear biblical principles. Mentoring Communities give space for resting
from activity. Mentoring Communities create environments where we
grow in love of each other and Christ and we come to know ourselves
better. The safe times, places, and people help us grow and flourish for
our life of ministry.

The press of the world will try to convince us that we are too busy to take a week a year to be apart with God and friends. I wonder, too, if sometimes we are afraid because we know we have already started down a path that will lead to no good end. These are the times when we especially need others to pull us back and to love and encourage us to walk in the full light of Christ.

There are also those of us who seriously do not believe they need anyone else. They can figure it out as they go. They have too much to do and have managed just fine on their own. The result of avoiding the support and accountability of a Mentoring Community might be empty ministries with little fruit, or empty relationships with others or with God, or an empty resolve to resist moral or ethical temptation. Mentoring Communities provide ongoing connection with others for prayer and support and create a yearly week to rest in God and recalibrate in a community with like-minded peers and a mentor.

Much of what I do with inner-city moms is mentoring. When I met Anne at the first Mentoring Community gathering, I was impressed that I learned less from formal teaching sessions but so much more from our life-together times . . . the casual conversations, the walks, and the seeing of Christ lived out practically in so many different lives. I would love to cultivate that presence of Jesus in my life so that it would overflow to the moms I work with.

CHRISTINE, URBANPROMISE
(CANADA)

Suggested Rhythm for Mentoring Communities

This schedule is based on a Mentoring Community that meets for five days with a lead mentor and eight other people. There are many variations on this schedule. This suggested schedule is an optimal rhythm for these types of gatherings. The practical logistics for starting and sustaining a Mentoring Community are found in the chapter following this one.

Day One

- Arrival
- Dinner together
- Review of time together

An arrival day allows people to come from various distances and from a variety of responsibilities. If travel is involved, giving a day for transportation creates a buffer for all between work, family, and the retreat time. Some people might need to work a full day. This way, when the group begins, no one will miss any part of the experience together.

Day Two

- Breakfast in silence
- Prayer and Bible reflection
- Group Listening Prayer
- Lunch in community
- Options for the afternoon
- Group Listening Prayer
- Dinner in community
- Evening prayer
- Bedtime

Breakfast in Silence (60 minutes): Beginning the day in silence gives everyone an opportunity to have a personal devotional time and collect themselves for the day. Leaders' typical days are full of conversations and meetings. Having silence at the beginning of the retreat prepares us to hear the Holy Spirit first, and it prepares our hearts to hear each other.

Prayer and Bible reflection (30 minutes): Usually, the mentor does the morning prayer and Bible reflection time. The opening time prepares the group for the day, so it is more reflective than active. In other words, it is not meant to be a teaching time or a time for the delivery of a message or sermon. Neither is it meant to be an Intercessory Prayer time, but a time of silent prayer and reflection. Often, the mentor will have a theme for the week together.

One year, I led a series of Bible reflections on the theme "Seeing as Jesus Sees." We read John 9:35-41 and considered our desire to see. The next day, we read various passages where Jesus said, "Come and see." For the third full day, we read Matthew 5:8 and 1 Corinthians 13:11-13, with the prayer "Lord, bless me with a pure heart to see you."

Another year, I led a devotional series on the phrase "Be here now" (the phrase survivalists teach people who go into the wilderness, to pay attention to where they are, not where they are trying to get to). For the "Be," I used John 15:1-11, which is about the importance of abiding in God's will. For the second day, I used Luke 24:13-34 and Psalm 1, which are about the importance of the "here" and using the senses to see God fully in the present moment. On the final full day, using Luke 12:24-34, we thought about how the worries of this world cause anxiety and separate us from the "now" of God's present help.

Group Listening Prayer (2 hours—60 minutes each for two people, with a break between): The heart of the Mentoring Community experience is Group Listening Prayer. It is the essential component that brings together listening to another and the Holy Spirit with praying for one another. Each person gets a full hour to share and be prayed for. Most people need at least thirty minutes to share, then listening to the Spirit, reporting, and praying for the individual who shared takes the other thirty minutes.

Since participants usually get together once a year, having at least thirty minutes gives the sharer adequate opportunity to tell the story of the past year and bring to the group the primary concern for which they need prayer this new year. The Group Listening Prayer is a combination of opening silence to prepare to listen, listening to the one sharing, then listening to the Holy Spirit, each sharing what they received from the Spirit, and a hands-on prayer for the one who shared. A small break of five to ten minutes is taken for using the bathroom or drinking and to give the group an opportunity to stretch before listening to another person. After the break, the second person shares, then the group takes another break.

> The opportunity to hear myself—and to get feedback from what the group is hearing—helps me listen to God's voice more clearly. I've struggled with focusing too much on myself (*How am I doing?*). As a lead pastor, I cannot realistically share openly about this inner wrestling, but I can do that in our gatherings. The group's insights help to focus myself more God-ward and less me-ward! My mentor is always a voice of affirmation. I feel like Timothy or Titus, encouraged by Paul to serve Christ with courage, even in difficult circumstances of ministry conflict.
>
> JONATHAN, CHURCH PLANTER (MEXICO)

Lunch in community (60 minutes for fellowship): Mealtimes are important times for connecting, updating, and having conversations. The logistics of mealtimes can vary from one place to another. If the group is staying at a retreat center, the meals are usually provided as part of the overall costs. If the group has rented a home or room, then meals can be catered or the group can do their own cooking. This requires a little more planning, but my group really enjoys the hospitality of cooking their favorite meals for each other. Breakfast might be simple items that individuals can prepare on their own, such as cereal or an egg and toast. Lunch might be the fixings for sandwiches or salads, which participants might prepare for themselves. One or two people must then take responsibility for shopping for these breakfasts and lunches. Costs are usually divided equally between everyone, but sometimes the costs are on a sliding scale, depending on financial capacities.

In the evening, participants can take turns preparing a special meal. In my group, we share the costs of breakfast and lunch but whoever cooks the evening meal takes responsibility for its cost. In some groups, everyone cooks and cleans together. Another group brought a person with them who volunteered to do all the cooking.

Options for the afternoon: Afternoons are usually open for a variety of possibilities, such as those listed below.

- *Silent retreat time for everyone:* We recommend that one afternoon be allotted for a time of silence and reflection. It is very helpful, especially on the first afternoon, to have a silent retreat time, where each person is encouraged to pray and reflect on their past year. Some groups begin with an extra day or morning just for silence and reflection, before any group activities begin. Some Mentoring Community participants have a special journal just for their yearly retreat away. This helpful practice allows each person to review what was shared in the previous year and what was recorded during their Group Listening Prayer time. They begin to see patterns, growth, and stuck places and to see the movement of God in their lives.

> *I came to the Mentoring Community time not really knowing what I was going to share this year. However, when I read over my Mentoring Community journal over the stretch of six years, I saw how faithful God had been and how much I had grown. I realized how stuck I was two years ago and then how fulfilled and free I feel in my ministry today. I decided to use my sharing time to make a history of God's faithfulness in my life.*
>
> JACOB, PASTOR (USA)

- *Group excursion:* Depending on where you hold your gathering, different excursions or outdoor activities are possible. Sometimes the retreat place has so many resources that going off the property isn't necessary. Many retreat centers have hiking paths and prayer walks. One group stayed at a house built by a businessperson who had a vision to create a place where ministers could relax and pray and escape from the pressures of ministry. The property included canoeing and kayaking opportunities, a pool, and a tennis court. Another group took hikes together. Another visited a museum and an art gallery. Another took time to explore the local sites in a city. Each excursion gave the participants an opportunity to be together in a different setting and to relax.

- *One-on-one conversations:* Another possible use of the afternoon time is for one-on-one conversations with the mentor and each participant. This gives the mentor an opportunity to hear more about each mentee's life and ministry and to ask spiritual questions. Personal time with the mentor also builds warm relationship bonds with the mentee.

Group Listening Prayer (another person—60 minutes): For groups of more than six people (three full days with two sharing each morning = six people), someone else needs to share in the afternoon or evening. Some groups prefer having another person after the evening meal, and others would rather have the evening open to decompress and have fun together, so they do a third person right after lunch or before dinner. The format is the same as for the morning Group Listening Prayer times.

Dinner in community: Logistics of the evening meal were discussed in the section

A year ago, Pablo had shared about struggles he was having with a coworker who continually undermined his work in the church. He would question his ideas and challenge the veracity of his reports. Yet during Group Listening Prayer, when it was his turn, he didn't mention this coworker at all. When we had our one-on-one time, I asked him how it was going with the coworker. He said he was embarrassed to bring up the same problem this year and the situation hadn't really changed. In our personal time, we had an opportunity to explore why this was continuing to happen and what his options might be. I also encouraged him to talk with his groupmates about it.

J., MENTOR (MEXICO)

on lunch. Some groups, including mine, have a book that they read together each year and then discuss during these dinners. The book usually relates to the theme that the mentor chose for the Bible reflection time, but it doesn't need to. Each year, I try to pick a book for my group that will provoke deeper thinking about spiritual growth, God's mission in the world, or some of the social problems that communities face. I sometimes give them a choice between three or four books, as I'm not sure what they have already read.

Another option is reading articles available online that have relevant topics or watching a relevant podcast or talk. To grow spiritually, the mind, heart, and behaviors are engaged. A book or podcast can help stimulate the mind, engage the heart, and then change behaviors.

Evening prayer (30 minutes): At the end of the day, it is good to reflect on what has happened for the individual and the community. We recommend the Prayer of Reflection, which considers where each one experienced the most light of Christ or joy and where each one experienced less of Christ's light or joy. The Prayer of Reflection, also called the Prayer of Examen, is discussed more fully in the chapter on prayer.

Bedtime: It is important that everyone go to bed at a reasonable time so all are refreshed and ready for the next day.

Days Three and Four

The next two days repeat the pattern of the day before.

- Group Listening Prayer for three more people
- Different afternoon activities (as suggested in Day Two)

Day Five (Departure)

A final day for departure gives ample time for people to pack and clean up, if necessary. Some groups have a final morning worship time with Communion and leave-taking blessings for everyone.

We also recommend that at breakfast, if possible, the group discuss how the time went for everyone. Having a small evaluation allows for corrections to be made or creative ideas to be entertained. It is also recommended that the group add to their calendars *before they leave* when and where the next Mentoring Community retreat will happen. We have found that this is the best policy. After a couple of years, my group decided to meet the first week of August, every year. This pattern became the norm and was a fixed time on everyone's calendar.

Here is the schedule my group uses each time it meets:

Day One—Arrival and dinner
Days Two–Four

- 8:00 a.m.—Breakfast on own and in silence
- 9:00 a.m.—Prayer and Bible reflection
- 9:30–11:30 a.m.—Group Listening Prayer (two people)
- 12:00–1:00 p.m.—Lunch
- 1:30–2:30 p.m.—Group Listening Prayer (one person)
- 2:30–5:30 p.m.—One-on-one with lead mentor and/or group excursion
- 6:30–7:30 p.m.—Dinner: book discussion
- 8:00–9:00 p.m.—Evening open
- 9:00–9:30 p.m.—Evening prayer

Day Five—Departure

Final Thoughts

Mentoring Communities can have a variety of schedules. This is the one we have used in Leighton Ford Ministries. In this book, we have focused on the normal schedule for a yearly Mentoring Community gathering.

I have tried to make it as clear as possible how a typical gathering works. This is a suggested pattern, though: It is up to each group to discover the format that works best for them. The above schedule works for nine people—eight participants and the mentor. Here are three other important considerations for the conclusion of this chapter:

- *The mentor*: Both the mentor and the participants share in Group Listening Prayer. The mentor is a full member of the community and is transparent about his or her life. Just as Jesus invited his disciples into his intimate world, so the mentor models authenticity and the movement of God for growth in their life.

- *The schedule balance*: A key component is balancing rest and activity. The Group Listening Prayer takes a central place in the days together. But it is also important to keep space in the days. The temptation in busy leaders' lives is to cram the Group Listening Prayer experience into two days and to omit as inconsequential silence, recreation, rest, and leisure. God is as much in the night as in the day, and as much in the silence as in the noise. God works and is as present in our rest and play as in our frenzied busyness—sometimes more so.

- *Group attentiveness*: If someone in the group is distracted and not attentive, it diminishes the experience for the entire group. If someone is not engaged and seems disinterested in the experience, it tarnishes the experience for everyone. Mentoring Communities do not work well unless everyone agrees to be fully attentive. So, what to do if someone is not? The mentor (or, if it is a peer group, some group member) talks to the individual to discern if they are ready for this type of experience. If a person is not fully present or is uninterested in this type of community, it is best not to invite them back.

During the Lausanne Younger Leaders Gathering in Jakarta, Indonesia, the first week of August 2016, the planning team wanted to make mentoring a core feature of the participants' seven-day experience. The Leighton Ford Ministries' Spiritual Mentoring training team brought in about twenty-five of their trained mentors, along with almost one hundred other seasoned leaders chosen by Lausanne. The one thousand younger leader participants from 120 countries were divided into diverse mentoring groups of six to eight people, with a lead mentor for each group.

Our Mentoring Training team met a day before the conference to train the additional one hundred seasoned leaders in Group Listening Prayer. The already trained mentors were dispersed in the group to model the process. When the participants arrived, they were given time to create a life map. A life map is a visual depiction on one page of paper (11×13) of the story of their life: the ups and downs, the momentous experiences, and the movement of God through their story. A life map is an expression of our identity and calling to love and serve Christ.

Every day, each mentoring group would meet with their mentor. The younger leaders assigned to the group would take turns sharing their life maps in a Group Listening Prayer format. Each participant had the full attention of everyone in their group and experienced the benefit of being fully listened to (without comment or input), then prayed for as the participants listened to the Holy Spirit. It was an extraordinary experience. Amid the busy conference with worship, plenary speakers, workshops, and one-on-one conversations, every participant was hosted as they told their story.

Many of the participants had never fully told their story to anyone and had never experienced the wonder of being listened to and prayed for. Some participants shared things that had never been spoken but that desperately needed to be. During one of those mentoring group times, when we were spread out all over the campus, my group was a few tables away from another group. We couldn't hear each other, of course, except for the murmuring of voices, but we could clearly see that the lead mentor was on his computer or talking on his phone the entire time. On that particular day, two younger leaders shared their maps and the older leader never looked up from his work or joined the group in prayer.

There is no gift more beautiful or generous than our attention to each other. When it is not there, our hearts close a little.

The Gifts We Offer and Receive in Mentoring Communities

God's grace comes to us in so many ways. As one Mentoring Community participant said about his own life: "It just comes!" So we embrace this Mentoring Community as a gift from God to us—one we share. Leighton asked members of his group what gifts the Mentoring Community has offered to them. Here are some of their responses:

Relationships grow deep and strong when you know someone will truly listen to you. When you are known for being a good listener and for asking good spiritual questions, people will trust you and open up to you. They will come to you not for your answers but for your safe presence. This creates a culture of trust where people can trust each other by being deep and vulnerable because they know someone's not going to try to "fix" them but will be silent and listen to God before offering any insightful words.

JEREMIAH, JEWS FOR JESUS (USA)

The gift of hospitality. "Setting a table to make us feel nourished. Not only in the place we meet but in open hearts, food lovingly prepared, places of beauty and loveliness to gather."

The gift of space for God. "This is not a vacation or just a reunion. I come to meet with God."

The gift of listening. "Of being honest—not just blurting things out but waiting for what shows up in the room."

The gift of cleansing and renewal. "A kind of spiritual scrub down."

The gift of trust. "And of exposure. We can take the risk of sharing the deepest things in our lives, knowing there is no competition but complete confidentiality."

The gift of story. "Over time, we get to know each other—the sacred stories about our lives. It is a place for transparency."

The gift of connecting. "With other like-minded people, networking. The peer-to-peer relationships are deeply valuable."

The gift of generosity. "Unlike many training programs that benefit the sponsoring group, this is one that gives without expectation of return. And it is made available without charge."

The gift of freedom. "Time to be in nature, to meet our own needs . . . a nap, a walk, coffee. Space for what we need to do—play, write, pray, think. Not completely programmed."

The gift of family. "Retreats are like a family reunion, a second family. I don't do anything else where I am so received and nourished."

Building and Sustaining a Mentoring Community

This past year, as we got ready to travel to our Mentoring Community,
we thought it would be our last, because of changes in our life
circumstances, finances, time commitments, and more. After the first
day of being together, we quickly determined that this community is our
cup of cold water and we will do whatever necessary to stay a part.

RICH AND ROSE, VINEYARD LEADERS (USA)

We want to be artists of the soul and friends on the journey.
LEIGHTON FORD

FROM THE VERY BEGINNING of developing Mentoring Communities,
I was involved with Leighton and others. Several of us were trying to
imagine how to replicate Leighton's Mentoring Community experiences
with his two groups for other mentors and leaders. We were all aware
that there was an urgency in the church and in mission for leaders who
lead like Jesus, to Jesus, and for Jesus. We were all aware that many leaders throughout the world were lonely and struggling to figure out their
callings and ministries without much support. We all wanted to develop
the next generation of Christian leaders into faithful, long-term, and
fruitful influencers for God's mission.

But I had a red flag: a series of related questions. Is this something
that works primarily for privileged Western people with resources of

time and finances? Does it also work in other countries and Christian cultures where time and money are thin? The life of a pastor in the Andes Mountains of Peru, where Randy and I worked for several years, is not the same as the life of a pastor in rural Iowa, even though both are in farming communities. Many pastors and leaders in India have to work full-time as well as pastor, a calling often coming without pay. In Ghana, the women leaders had full-time jobs as well as the responsibilities of caring for their children and families. Would they have the time and the money to do this?

Another series of questions for me were around the elements of the Mentoring Community experiences. Would they respond to the silence and to reflective prayer and reflective Bible study? Would Listening Prayer and listening to each other and the Spirit feel meaningful to them, in how their spiritual lives are activated in God? Do they also feel a need for peer companionship and reflection? Is this a human desire or a privileged one?

When we began to get invitations from other parts of the world to train potential leaders to be mentors and start Mentoring Communities, I was eager to be involved. I traveled to Cape Town, India, Singapore, Indonesia, Kenya, and Ghana. Others trained in Mexico and Thailand, as well as Europe, Canada, and Australia. I also had lengthy conversations about Mentoring Communities with leaders from all over the world, including Brazil, Tanzania, Egypt, Zambia, Pakistan, Nepal, Botswana, China, Cambodia, and Russia.

What I discovered compelled me to write this book with Leighton and Anne. First, everywhere I traveled, I found that leaders young and old were hungry for companionship. They were lonely. They also wanted to find ways to encourage and train developing leaders not to be superstars but to be ordinary, faithful leaders following Jesus' example.

Second, in the same way everywhere, everyone responded to the extraordinary gift of silence, openness, Listening Prayer, and friend conversations. And third, what surprised me most was that the experience of Mentoring Communities made such a profound difference in individuals' lives that groups found ways to make it happen. Time and financial resources were worked out.

A few years ago, I was training a group of leaders from southern African countries in Karen, Kenya. At the end of the training is a question-and-answer time. Always, the question of finances comes up. How do you pay for the place

There are ways that Africans get at the internal world and bring it up, so I wanted to know—Is this Western or African? It is true that issues have come out during my Mentoring Community experience in Karen. Then this can only be a Christian-culture experience. This crosses cultures. You lay down bare and face your darkness. This is Christian.

WILFRED, EVANGELIST AND PASTOR (TANZANIA)

and food and travel of a yearly, five-day Mentoring Community experience? They began brainstorming options, when someone suggested that they could tap into their Western resources for money. At that point, Bishop John, a man highly respected in Kenya for his servant leadership and deep faith, said in a loud voice, "If this is about asking for money from mission organizations, I want no part of it. If this is from God, we can do this."

The Krupa (Grace) group of women leaders from eastern Asia have been meeting faithfully together annually since 2012, and several have started groups in their own countries. One of the women makes her own paper and designs greeting cards to sell to pay for her flight. Another woman sells eggs from her chickens. They set a date and put aside money so they can be together. And they find very reasonable places to stay.

So, I believe in this, and I believe it is not a special experience for a privileged few but the experience that brothers and sisters all over the world need to lead faithfully with companions and to thrive for the long haul of ministry. This chapter is dedicated to the important, practical questions that are related to developing successful Mentoring Communities.

Before we start responding to questions, we want to say again that Mentoring Communities are not so much about style as about substance.

We are surprised at the variety and creativity people use to put together Mentoring Communities. We have presented a model in this book, yet we know different models exist and almost every question has been answered a different way. The style is up to the mentor and the context.

The substance is always our concern. Mentoring Communities are about listening to each other and the Spirit, praying, and being in community together for the long haul. They do not replace church fellowship, small groups, or spiritual directors, counselors, and coaches. Mentoring Communities are for leaders who want support and care outside of the press of their ministry responsibilities and the constraints of their contexts.

How Do You Describe the Mentoring Community?

Mentoring Communities help leaders thrive and mature for the duration of ministry. Jesus himself gathered developing leaders and mentored them in community. Mentoring Communities follow that example by creating safe times, safe places, and safe people for a group of leaders to grow spiritually in the care of a mentor.

A group commits to regular times of going apart to places where they are not distracted. In the companionship of a mentor and peers, they tell their stories, listen to each other, pray, fellowship together, and rest. This practice has a transforming impact on their spiritual vitality for the lifetime of their callings.

We are called to serve as *a community of friends on the journey*—followers, companions, and learners—together in the way of Christ.

- We are *followers* of Christ as our leader, guided by the Spirit, on the way home to the Father.
- We are *companions* with those who seek to lead like Jesus and to lead others to him.
- We are *learners* helping each other grow in the art of Spiritual Mentoring (or companionship).

How Are People Selected for the Mentoring Community?

From the beginning, we urge young men and women to be "Kingdom seekers, not empire builders." In our mentoring, we have been looking for Kingdom-seeking leaders, *men and women who have a passion to lead for Jesus, like Jesus, and to Jesus.*

Many years ago, Leighton took a page from the example of Oswald Sanders, an outstanding mission statesman of his time. Sanders kept a list of younger people whom he sensed had strong leadership potential, so that he could encourage them. Leighton began what he called his own "GGTW" list—Guys and Gals to Watch.

> When I felt particularly drawn to someone, I added them to the list, prayed for them, kept in touch by calls and letters, and invited them to spend a day together and occasionally, to join me in ministry. From that list came our first mentoring group—the "Point Group." Group members came from different parts of the world. The distinctive focus of their ministry varied. So did their personalities and styles.[1]

Each mentor/leader has to find the best way to do this. Typically, a group is chosen from people with whom the leader already has a mentoring relationship or a spiritual friendship. Chemistry between the mentor and peers is hard to describe, but it is very important. Most important is to invite those who have an open, seeking spirit, a desire to grow personally and in leadership, and a mind-set to listen, learn from others, and be Christlike in caring for others' interests.

We suggest you create a list of possible people and spend time in prayer and discernment about whether to invite each person. A one-on-one conversation can help the mentor discern if the person is ready for a group such as this. Some Mentoring Community mentors have waited a year or more to prayerfully discern whom God is calling to be part of this experience.

Some of us have created groups from the recommendations of other leaders, and these have worked well too.

What If There Are No Mentors?

This question was briefly addressed in chapter 3, and it is true that there are large areas of the world where mentoring is an uncommon idea. In those cultures, the leaders have had to figure it out for themselves, so they expect that the next generation of leaders will do the same. But denomination and mission leaders everywhere are finding that the next generation is asking for more of an investment in their development beyond just more education.

If there are no mentors, peers can decide that they want to create a Mentoring Community for themselves. Having a mentor is not a requirement. Hopefully, this book gives enough information to assist anyone in creating a Mentoring Community.

Do You Recommend Groups Be Made Up of People from the Same Ministry or Locale?

Generally not. For one thing, Spiritual Mentoring may not be as helpful and open if the leader is also the boss. Also, people may not speak as freely if the other members live or work too closely to them. But different forms of Mentoring Communities have developed in churches or denominations. There is a group of church planters and pastors in Mexico that meet once a month for Group Listening Prayer, and they also take a weekend trip annually.

What Kind of Commitment Is Involved in Joining a Mentoring Community?

We suggest asking group members to meet one time initially, with the understanding that after that first meeting, the group can decide if they wish to continue. If so, they are asked to commit to meet annually for at least three years. After that, they are asked to make an ongoing commitment.

Each group member agrees to make the annual retreat a priority—to come on time and not leave early except for emergencies. We tell each person, "Don't make the group retreat an option. Treat the dates the same way you would if you were attending a conference where you were a central speaker. You are not casual about the commitment." It is helpful to review and update the group commitment from time to time.

What Is the Ideal Size?

About eight to ten members. With more than that, it becomes difficult to allow ample sharing time. With fewer than that, if some people have to miss, the dynamic changes. But there is no hard-and-fast rule. Some larger groups break into smaller groups of four for Group Listening Prayer.

How Important Is It That the Mentoring Communities Be Diverse?

Quite important. With members engaged in different ministries and various cultural settings, the cross-fertilization is very valuable. Similarly, a group is enriched by having members with different personalities. Blending those who tend to be activists with others more given to contemplative reflection helps all grow in their love for the fullness of Christ's body. In today's global context, the more diverse the community, the better we appreciate the church universal as Christ's bride. The more diverse the members, the more likely the group can spiritually grow into Christ's likeness.

> I have been greatly encouraged by the authenticity and transparency of the group to live out an authentic, noncompartmentalized Christian life in all aspects. Realizing that all of us go through similar experiences, temptations, struggles, and issues helps me know that I am not alone. . . . The support of close peers around the world who are praying for me gives me confidence to continue. The spiritual direction of my mentor and the peer-to-peer mentoring of friends is one of my most treasured yearly experiences. Our group is truly an iron-sharpens-iron experience.
>
> STEPHEN, SENIOR PASTOR (PHILIPPINES)

Is It Better for Groups to Be Mixed Gender or of the Same Sex?

That depends. Most of the groups we know include both men and women. Several, however, have only men or only women. In some cultures, same-sex groups are necessary. To a great extent, this depends on the leader, their circle of ministry, and the need. We do think, in today's world, that there is great value in men and women in ministry getting to know each other well and be comfortable with each other. As one woman said, "I mentor men in my ministry. And I have learned so much from the men in our group." The same is true of men learning from the women present. At the same time, there can be great value for women to meet, since so often, their contribution is undervalued. In some of our long-term groups, spouses have occasionally been included.

What about Groups Including Married Couples?

If both the spouses are active in leadership and ministry, Mentoring Communities with spouses can work well, but we have some reservations. For one thing, these are not meant as marriage-enrichment groups. From experience with trying married-couple groups, we found it didn't work particularly well, partly because of scheduling problems of having both parents away if there are children at home. Perhaps the criterion should be that both spouses are actively involved in ministry leadership, whether separately or together, and both highly desire this sort of gathering. In some cultures, such as in part of the evangelical culture in India, spouses go together to almost all ministry-related events. In the Mentoring Community I am familiar with in southern India, the couples meet together but the men and women split into separate groups for Group Listening Prayer.

What If a Person Doesn't Work Out in the Community?

Every now and then, a person doesn't work out in a Mentoring Community. Sometimes the problem is a personality clash between the person and the rest of the group. Sometimes the person is too busy to make the retreat time a priority, so they rarely come. Sometimes the person just isn't that interested. One mentor told of having a person in their group who would wander off to read a book or do work and wouldn't come to the Group Listening Prayer times. I heard of another group where one of the individuals was constantly provoking arguments with others about his political views. Mentoring Communities are not political forums. They are sacred spaces for spiritual companionship and growth.

If a person clearly isn't working out in the community, and the mentor has tried to address the issue with the individual one-on-one and it hasn't made a difference, then the person isn't invited back. Mentoring Communities must be safe places with safe people. If a person isn't safe, then they aren't ready for this type of community. If a person isn't safe, they also aren't ready to listen and learn.

How Does the Mentor Manage a Group If Someone Talks Too Much?

Every group needs a person to guide the process for creating the group's harmony. Mentors manage the environment so it is a safe place and time with safe people. Mentoring Communities are powerful precisely because they can help us grow as leaders when we are in intimate community with each other. Sometimes, individuals are not aware of the amount of "space" they are taking up by talking too much. It is the mentor's responsibility to manage the time and the talking so that everyone gets an equal amount of time during Group Listening Prayer.

When a person talks too much, the mentor can remind them that time is running out. The mentor can speak privately to the person about taking up too much space. In an inexperienced group, where people are beginning to learn about each other and develop trust, the mentor can set a timer for an allotted time that each group member will share. With a mature group, the time is more fluid. Some people need a lot of time, perhaps two hours, to unpack their stories (maybe a spouse died or a ministry collapsed), while others only need thirty minutes because they had fewer changes or challenges in their past year.

Who Leads the Mentoring Community? Who Handles All the Details?

In the beginning, the mentor often manages the details. But we recommend that the mentor team up with someone who will help them with the details. Usually, the mentor knows another person who really enjoys providing support. Or two mentors can work together to start a group.

Details involve communication about plans and transportation, a place for the retreat, meals, excursions, and anything extra that would help the experience go well, such as weather forecasts and what to pack. In the beginning, smooth organization really helps create a welcoming environment. In my group, Space4Grace, I send an invitation letter with all the details about travel, schedule, food assignments, dress, and book focus. Today, after eleven years together, my group handles most of the details among themselves, and I give my energy to leading the group. Groups usually move from mentor-led to peer-organizing communities.

How Do Mentoring Communities Pick a Time and Place, or Plan Food and Excursions?

Once a community is established, the last meal together or the last Group Listening Prayer session is a good time for the group to decide when and where it will meet next and who will take point on organizing different elements. Most communities have found that selecting the same time every year works best. Then the days are set aside on the calendar a year ahead to avoid conflict with other things that might arise.

What Is Recommended for the First Gathering?

The first time the community gathers is an important time. Usually, people don't fully understand what they have been invited to because they haven't experienced it. Therefore, some discussion and basic training—especially around listening and Group Listening Prayer—are very helpful. The mentor can explain, model, and guide the process, giving more direction at the beginning to help everyone understand how it works. We also recommend that the first time the group gathers, each member tell their personal and spiritual story to the group as a way to really get to know everyone.

> When I meet with my mentor and ministry peers, it is a wonderful opportunity to reflect on my story and find God in fresh and surprising ways. It is extremely energizing to journey with my brothers and sisters in Christ through their ongoing stories and to be surprised with them as we uncover God's incredible work. When I want to quit, I am encouraged by those journeying with and ahead of me. This is my real-life great "cloud of witnesses" that cheers me on, gives me perspective, reminds me that God is ever with me [Hebrews 12:1].
>
> MICHELLE, PASTOR (USA)

How Are Mentoring Communities Financed?

There are as many financial models as there are types of Mentoring Communities. Sometimes the mentor raises money to help with some of the expenses of the first gathering. Sometimes a sponsor wants to provide resources for leaders to have this kind of community. Sometimes a church or denomination or grant provides the resources. Other times, the members do what they need to do to raise the money for their journey to the yearly Mentoring Community retreat. Sometimes some group members have more resources than others, so they gift money for other members' expenses. Church leaders often use their continuing education funding to cover expenses.

I have seen the very poor find a way to be together in a tiny place, sleeping eight people in one room in bunk beds and cooking together in order to make the gathering affordable for all. For them, the joy was loving and serving each other with companionship and prayer. The Krupa (Grace) are women who have always served and have rarely been served. They find a way to get together. They inspire me to trust the Lord to provide the resources we need each year for our gathering because it has such a profound impact on our souls.

How Do Mentoring Communities Stay in Touch the Rest of the Year?

Not all effective mentoring happens in set times and places. A lot of mentoring happens in "small touches." Often, a thirty-minute walk or a fifteen-minute phone call may be significant for someone.

I recall some long, late-evening phone conversations with two different young leaders. Each was on the verge of losing either their ministry or their marriage because of the stress of disappointment, fatigue, and criticism. In both cases, God used a listening ear and heart and some encouraging words to hold out hope, and today, both are in even stronger and deeper ministries.

Social media offers many ways for groups to stay in touch and continue the safe place, time, and people environment. Some Mentoring Communities have a WhatsApp group. Just this morning, in a closed WhatsApp group, I read the blessings and reports from a recent gathering in Ghana. Some groups create a private Facebook page. Others use an email group to check in with each other each month.

The lead mentor can stay in touch with text, email, or a phone call with a brief word of encouragement, Scripture, or prayer. As the group matures, they naturally stay in touch with each other, alerting the community to prayer needs or upcoming events. Leighton Ford reflects on this dynamic:

> Frank Laubach used to speak of "flash prayers" he would direct toward someone, even perhaps a stranger on a train, when so moved in his spirit. I find myself doing that, perhaps on a walk when my mind is receptive and a particular person pops into my mind. Sunday mornings, I often go "around the world" in quiet prayer, from Sydney to Singapore, and Vancouver to Marburg, and spots in between, praying for members of our mentoring groups as they minister that day.

Can the Schedule Be Different? Can Mentoring Communities Work with Other Trainings or in a Church?

Usually, Mentoring Communities meet for retreats once a year for four to six days, each with its own lead mentor. But no one pattern or style fits all Mentoring Communities. Each one reflects the personality and gifts of the mentor leader, and each is fashioned to serve a diverse group of mentees. The members are engaged in various ministries, yet all have a strong commitment to serve Christ. They are at different stages in their lives and ministries. Their needs vary from time to time and year to year.

Some groups are more spontaneous in how they spend time together, others more structured. There is freedom in the Spirit to be faithfully creative. Some churches are trying Mentoring Communities with their staff or with their discipleship groups.

There is no one pattern for a retreat, but Group Listening Prayer and authentically paying attention to each individual are always at the core. The elements of a retreat may differ. Retreats may include times of listening to the Word, journaling, prayer walks, listening to and writing poetry, centering prayer, learning (as artists of the soul) to see in new ways, times of silence and waiting, freewriting, silence during meals while listening to a reading—and times of games and play! Again, however, while styles differ, we are committed to three vital aspects in our Spiritual Mentoring:

- attention to whole-life development;
- withdrawing together for a time, yearly; and
- commitment to long-term (ideally, lifelong) relationships.

If I Have More Questions or Want to Connect to Other Mentoring Communities, What Can I Do?

With this book, our prayer is that Mentoring Communities might be created anywhere the desire and need are apparent to mentors or leaders.

183

The book should offer enough guidance to allow anyone to start their own Mentoring Community.

If you have more questions or want to share about your group and ask for prayer, you can contact us at https://www.leightonfordministries.org/. Leighton Ford Ministries is a group of people mentored and inspired by Leighton Ford who want to unite leaders in Mentoring Communities.

A Mentoring Community Story

To end this chapter, Leighton Ford describes a recent retreat with one of his Mentoring Communities.

I have been meeting with this group now for about fifteen years. Currently, there are eight members, five men and three women, most of them now in their mid-to-late forties. One is Canadian; one ministers in Africa; the rest are based in the United States. Several have been or are pastors. One is involved in ministry education. Another mobilizes missionary movements on another continent.

I had a personal relationship with each member before inviting them to form a group. We met for the first time to explore the idea of an annual gathering, and since then, we have been committed to meet once a year. Three others were part of the initial gathering. One chose not to join because he belonged to another, similar peer group. Two dropped out for personal reasons and priorities. One of the commitments is to make this group a priority.

For this retreat, we met in a large, old North Carolina mountain home of friends who have made it available without charge each year. While we have occasionally met in a more institutional setting, we much prefer the informality and warmth of a home.

Two or three people arrive early for an extra day of rest, but our official start is Monday evening, with dinner prepared by group members. After dinner, we sit inside by the fire and talk informally, bringing each other up to date about recent happenings and talking about plans for the week.

I remind them that our practice is to *not* fill the days too full—a mistake we made in the early years of our retreats. "So take time to sleep and relax and just to be together." We end the evening with a simple Compline Prayer from the Book of Common Prayer, which I lead with one of the members.

The next morning, members rise when they wish and prepare their own breakfast. As we gather together about 9:00, we begin with Morning Prayer, again from the Book of Common Prayer. Now it is time to begin our Group Listening Prayer. We agreed on time allotments to make sure all had a chance to share and be prayed for.

"Who will go first?"

"I am here," says Elizabeth. We all respond, "We see you. Welcome." This is a traditional greeting we have adopted from a southern African tribe, which uses those words to welcome a tribal member home from a journey.

Elizabeth, a pastor and evangelist, a wife and mother, shares with us about her ministry, but mostly about her children, including her anxiety about a daughter whose knee has been badly damaged during surgery. When she is through sharing, we pray for her concerns and some people gather around her with gentle touches.

So goes the morning. One after another speaks as they are led, with no prescribed order, as they will continue to do the next day. Two people tell about critical passages in their marriages. One is on a yearlong sabbatical and study leave after ending a difficult pastorate. Another is facing conflict in his denominational relations. Still another rejoices in his small son and the growth of his church in a very secular Canadian city. One of the women reports with pain how she feels totally unnoticed by her leader yet is excited about the evangelistic trips she takes to remote villages in Africa.

Although we have been apart a year, we have an immediate sense of rapport and understanding. Each person comes from a different place, yet all share the same desire—to live holy and humane lives—and all need the support and prayers of the others. This Spiritual Mentoring group remembers, and in a sense sings, each other's song—whether of lament or praise.

The group knows my song too. The third morning, it is my time to share. This year mine is a song of loss and lament. Two longtime friends have died, one of the first young men I mentored is seriously ill, and I have been through a case of shingles (thankfully gone). I speak of not having my own pastor at some critical times and of the loneliness that can come to senior leaders. I am not only a mentor; I, too, am cared for by the group and need this time with them.

After a light lunch, afternoons are totally free for participants to do as they most need—take a nap, run or walk, have a conversation over coffee, read. What we ask they *not* do is to spend the whole time catching up on email or making calls or preparing messages. Slowing down the mind is vital to opening the heart. For some, this is a very difficult rule!

Before dinner, we sit by the outdoor fireplace, cool drinks in hand and warm wraps around our shoulders, just being together. Later, we share dinner, either making it ourselves (some preparing, some cleaning up) or perhaps eating out one night.

The evening times vary. This year, one of the group has asked that we read Kathleen Norris's *Acedia and Me*, an updated reflection on the "eighth bad thought"—what ancient monks called "the noonday demon."[2] We talk about that jaded sense of disinterest in spiritual things—or anything—that can afflict us in the middle years of life. (The year before, we read Margaret Guenther's meditations on Psalm 62, *My Soul in Silence Waits*, and used a chapter daily to stir our reflections.)

A final shared prayer, Compline, ends our day together. Some watch a movie. Others go to bed early. Some stay up talking until after midnight. We depart on Friday morning, all with a sense of grace received and companions we will miss. But we will call and email throughout the year (some more than others), and next year, we'll come together again in Canada.

Afterword

My Mentoring Story

Written by Leighton Ford

Leaders in ministry need safe times, safe places, and safe people to keep going for the long run.

AS I LOOK BACK OVER the six decades since I was ordained as an evangelist, I am grateful for each phase of my ministry journey. It has unfolded in three stages, each flowing into the other. Stage one was as a worldwide preaching evangelist. Stage two involved drawing evangelism and mission leaders together in cooperation. Stage three has been one of identifying and mentoring emerging leaders around the world.

My own mentoring story began long before I knew I was being mentored or even knew the word. It began and has continued by encountering remarkable mentors. It has grown through times of deep pain. And it has brought great fulfillment through the grace of meeting and mentoring promising younger leaders.

The best way for me to tell this story is through key figures and times in my life.

Stage One—Worldwide Preaching Evangelist

Abandonment and Invitation

I was fourteen years old, and the year had been very hard, yet became encouraging.

My adopted mother, Olive, who was both devout and troubled, had left early in the year from our hometown of Chatham, Ontario, to live in Winnipeg, Manitoba, under an assumed name. I later realized she was suffering from severe paranoia, afraid that my father, who was her partner in their jewelry store, was going to harm her in some way.

Mom came back in late spring, but that sense of being left alone stayed with me.

That summer, a new Bible conference opened nearby, and I went with some friends. I liked the other young people there and was moved by that week's speaker, Oswald Smith. He told us how, since he was nervous and easily distracted, he prayed by walking up and down, praying out loud, and turning verses from the Psalms into words of prayer.

The next morning, I took my Bible into the nearby woods and prayed in the way he described. I don't remember the Scripture verses that spoke to me. I do remember sensing God's presence and care for this lonely fourteen-year-old.

That September, 1946, a man came to Chatham to promote the Canadian Youth Fellowship, a forerunner of Youth for Christ. Evon Hedley looked more like an executive than a preacher. He inspired a small group of us, meeting in a storefront church, to organize youth rallies to reach our friends for Christ.

My friend Danny nominated me as president, and Evon confirmed the appointment. He had assumed I was seventeen, because I was tall. When he found out I was only fourteen, he must have nearly had a heart attack!

But Evon stuck with us—and with me. He sent speakers our way. Gave me ideas. Set up my first speaking opportunities. Took me to national conferences and introduced me to the leaders. He scolded me once when I didn't show up for an appointment. Later, after I began my ministry of evangelism, he introduced me to people who would become lifelong teammates.

I didn't know that Evon was "mentoring" me. But he was a "way opener" for this young lad. As I write (in 2017), Evon is 101 years old, lives in Southern California, and still mentors younger men!

Disappointment and Prayer

It's a cold, icy southern Ontario night. The roads are frozen over. But despite the weather, the largest crowd ever to attend one of our local Youth for Christ rallies has packed our vocational-school auditorium.

They have come from miles around to hear a young evangelist from the southern United States, Billy Graham, who is already well known for his forceful, dynamic messages.

We have put up posters all over the county, sent word around to the churches, and put ads in the paper. We have prayed long and hard and invited all our friends who, as far as we know, are not true "Christians." We are sure that for many of them, this night will be their time to make a decision for Christ.

Billy's message does not disappoint. With a long, pointing finger, dramatic gestures, a piercing voice, and long, stretched-out southern syllables, he warns, "Prepaa . . . hhh to meet thy God."

He gives his invitation to come forward in commitment. The piano plays. We sing. He waits.

No one comes. He waits. Commands again, "You come." No one does. There is a painful silence. We shift in our seats. Pray more. Still no one comes. Finally, one twelve-year-old timidly walks to the front to rededicate her life to the Lord.

Billy prays for her. It's over. People leave.

I am devastated. I needn't have been, for that young girl later served the Lord in ministry. But we had expected everyone to respond. Cold, reserved Canadians that we were, public displays of faith were difficult. I knew that. But still, it wasn't what I had hoped for.

As the crowd left, I went to the wings of the stage and stood in the curtains by myself, close to tears. Then I felt an arm around my shoulder. It was Billy Graham. He had seen my disappointment, and he came over to encourage me.

"Leighton," he said, "I believe God has given you a burden to see people come to Christ. If you stay humble, I believe God will use you. I am going to pray for you."

That arm around the shoulder has stayed with me, as have those words of encouragement across the years, as I have passed on to younger leaders what I received.

After the meeting, at our home, Billy recommended I consider attending Wheaton College. Neither of us realized that was where I would meet and fall in love with his sister. Jeanie and I married while I was in seminary, and after graduation, Billy invited me to join his crusade team for a year, which stretched into thirty years of worldwide ministry, probably longer than he intended!

During those years, he was a mentor to me, not so much in a close-up relationship but in the example he set and the doors he opened. Often, he would invite me to sit in on a private luncheon with some church or civic leaders, and I saw how he would graciously weave faith into the conversation. He also trusted me with some demanding assignments.

In the fall of 1956, Billy's team was preparing for his first major crusade in New York City's Madison Square Garden the following summer. He called me up to his home in Montreat and said he wanted me to go to New York City to help prepare the way. I was to be the key contact with pastors and church leaders across the whole metropolitan area, sharing the vision of how the crusade could help their churches in their outreach. I was twenty-four years old, with absolutely no experience in that role. Seminary had not prepared me for such a task. Looking back, I wonder: If I had been him, facing the challenge of his largest crusade to date in the nation's largest city, would I have entrusted such a major responsibility to a young guy like me?

His early arm around the shoulder was a symbol of how he so often opened doors for me across thirty years—encouraging me to form a team and evangelize across my native Canada and in other countries, inviting me to deliver the message on the *Hour of Decision* broadcast with him every other week, recommending me to speak at special events and serve on some influential boards.

The time also came, in my older years, when he believed that because of changes coming in his organization, it was time for me to leave and begin a new ministry myself. He had opened many doors. Now he closed that one. And the closing of that door was the best thing that could have happened when it did.

When Jeanie and I visited him at his home in the North Carolina Mountains in 2017, I put my arm around his own shoulder. I did so gently, because at the time, he was ninety-six, frail, sight and hearing impaired, and sensitive to unexpected touches.[1]

"Billy," I said, as clearly as I could, "I want to thank you for what you meant to me as a boy in Canada, and across the years. Your arm around my shoulder so many years ago I will always remember."

I hoped he could hear me. There was a long pause. Then, quietly, he said, "Praise the Lord."

Stage Two—Drawing Evangelism and Mission Leaders Together

Passing On Leadership

In 1974, I had served as program chair for the International Congress on World Evangelization held in Lausanne, Switzerland. Initiated by Billy Graham, it was sponsored by a representative group of world leaders. *Time* magazine reckoned it was the largest gathering of evangelical leaders ever convened.[2] A committee of seventy-five members was appointed to follow up on the impact of this global event and to stimulate cooperation in world evangelization. "Lausanne" went beyond the event to become a vision and a movement to further the total biblical mission of the church.

The respected executive chairman of the congress, Anglican bishop

Jack Dain of Sydney, Australia, was also the first chair of the continuing Lausanne Movement. Jack was a veteran missionary leader in India. He was a skilled and experienced chair of many global committees, and he was also a close friend and confidant of Billy. He was respected around the world. And when he needed to step aside because of other heavy responsibilities, the seventy-five-member committee wondered who would replace him.

A nominating committee asked for names to be considered, and the regional groups all suggested that I succeed Jack as chair. They asked me to serve in part because they knew me as program chair for the 1974 congress. I also suspect it was in part because I came from Canada, a smaller nation known for diplomacy.

But I knew I would need help and guidance. And it came—from the retiring chair, Jack Dain himself. It's not always easy for an older leader to pass over the reins. In Jack's case, it was more than passing over a position. It was staying on in a lesser role.

Jack Dain was a man of tremendous stature and talent. I think he could have been secretary-general of the United Nations. But when he came (as he did for many more years) to the meetings of the Lausanne Committee, he virtually became my assistant. He would ring the bell to start the meetings. Bring me a glass of water. Let me know of any problems or disagreements in the group. He ran interference as needed and made suggestions about procedure (but only when asked). And most of all, he let me know I had his full confidence, support, and prayers.

In those years, I often needed to fly to Australia. The flights arrived about 6:00 a.m. Jack would always be waiting. He would insist, over my objections, on carrying my suitcase, even though he was twenty years older than I.

Jack embodied Jesus' value of the elder serving the younger and has been a model for my own mentoring. He became a father in the Lord to me. He had lovely daughters but no son; in a sense, I became that son, and I felt cared for as a son does by a father.

A few weeks before Jack died, I flew to his home in the south of

England. As I sat by his bed, I asked him which of all his ministries across the years meant most to him. Without a pause, he said, "Being a pastor to the six hundred clergy in Sydney." When I quoted Jesus' words in John 10:16 about the "other sheep" that needed to be found, Jack broke in and in a weak voice finished the sentence: "Them also I must bring."

With Jack, I felt more than a sheep. I felt like a son. Sometimes, in a quandary, I still stop, look up, and ask, "Jack, what would you do?" And often, I think I can sense what his wise answer would be.

Stage Three—Identifying and Mentoring Emerging Leaders

A Loss and a Legacy

In the fall of 1981, our beloved twenty-one-year-old son Sandy died during surgery at Duke University Medical Center to correct a problem with the electrical system of his heart. His death was totally unexpected, and shattering.

Two months later, I was on a flight I dreaded to take, the long haul from North Carolina to Sydney, Australia. I dreaded it not so much because of the time and distance involved but because of the separation from home and family and the huge hole in my heart with the loss of Sandy. Sandy was not only our oldest son but also a leader for Christ at his university, with a deep desire to serve the Lord in the years to come. He was full of dreams, and so were the expectations Jeanie and I had for him.

Leaving home for a long trek had always been difficult. But this time was so hard because the wound was fresh and grievous. I did not want to leave home. Yet I had promised to speak at an evangelism outreach on the north side of Sydney, and I had to go.

On that flight, halfway between the United States and Australia, I was musing about the future. I realized how many gray hairs there were among the leaders in the Lausanne Movement. And I wrote in my journal, "Perhaps the next thing is to bring together the emerging young leaders of the world."

In Sydney, I asked my friend Bishop John Reid whom he saw as future bishops in his diocese. "I can think of many blokes in their thirties," he said, "but not many in their forties who are leader material."

In my travels, I had already noticed a leadership gap apparent in the Christian world. Many key leaders who emerged after World War II and who had founded significant ministries were in their sixties and coming toward the close of their roles. At the same time, I had met a number of young leaders in their thirties who had fresh new visions. Between those generations, it seemed there were many managers, but not many leaders.

For the last two years, Jeanie and I had sensed that there might be a change in the direction of my ministry. We had begun a memorial fund after Sandy's death, one providing educational scholarships to help other young men and women go to seminary and prepare to run their race for Christ. In our hearts, we had a desire for other sons and daughters, not to replace Sandy but to pursue their own callings. And we were praying for clarity in our own calling.

A New Thing Springs Forth

During a time of prayer at one of our Lausanne Committee meetings, someone quoted the words of Isaiah: "Do not remember the former things, or consider the things of old. I am about to do a new thing; now it springs forth, do you not perceive it?" (Isaiah 43:18-19).

Those words were like an arrow to my heart. The prophet's words were to and about ancient Israel. But they also were words for Jeanie and me. I had been involved in preaching evangelism or gathering and leading evangelists through Lausanne for thirty years. They were wonderful and fulfilling years. I knew I would always be an evangelist, making Christ known. But now I had a new call.

The direction of this new calling was becoming clear. Losing a son led to a desire to nurture other young men and women, the emerging generation of young leaders around the world. The memory of that arm around the shoulder from Billy Graham so many years before inspired me to do for young leaders as he did for me. All these were coming together into forming a new ministry.

"Does anyone dare despise this day of small beginnings?" wrote the prophet Zechariah (Zechariah 4:9, MSG). Leighton Ford Ministries certainly began small. For years, I had been speaking to very large crowds. We had a sizable support and ministry team, and there had been a fair amount of publicity.

When we launched the new ministry in 1986, there were only my family and I, my longtime associate Irv Chambers, a small board, a few advisers, and a handful of prayer supporters.

Christianity Today raised the question as to what I was doing and described the new ministry as a transition "from mass evangelist to soul friend." In many ways, it was "like [my] former calling—but more personal."[3] It was up close, rather than at a distance from the pulpit or chair position. And it was certainly on a smaller scale.

One day, in a time of prayer and silent listening, I sensed strongly that God was saying, *If you want to make a difference, it will happen not through multiplying programs but by investing in people.* I wrote that sentence in a notebook that I have kept ever since.

Below, I wrote a list of men and women who came to mind, young leaders with potential and a heart for others and for the Lord. Remembering that the missionary leader Oswald Sanders kept a list of "blokes to watch," this became what I called my "GGTW list"—Guys and Gals to Watch.

The first ones were from half a dozen countries and were involved in a variety of ministries. I began to pray for them. I called them from time to time. I invited them to Charlotte for a day or two of conversation. I took them along on my ministry travels. Eventually, they and others became part of our first mentoring group—our "Point Group." A few years later, I invited a second mentoring group.

The pattern of these mentoring groups has been very simple: Once a year, we gather for a retreat. In the beginning, we took turns meeting near where each one lived and ministered. More recently, we gather each year in the North Carolina Mountains.

Early on, I invited some outside person to lecture. But soon we found the most valuable time was simply to be together. So our pattern is now the same. Each day, we begin with simple worship. In the mornings, group members have extended time to share where they are in their lives and ministries. We gather around each other in a circle of prayer. In the afternoons, we walk, run, rest, have fun, or simply relax together. In the evenings, after a long, relaxed dinner, there is time to talk about whatever is on our minds and in our hearts.

These retreats are a priority for each member. Each one understands that they are to make their participation as serious a priority as they would if they were the main speaker for the week.

We have been meeting annually now for many years. A few have dropped out. Some have been added. One woman survived serious cancer, another man lost a son through addictions, a third died with lung cancer after years of effective ministry as a pastor in Australia. Two have lost spouses.

Many have moved into significant national and international leadership roles. Others have faithfully ministered in the same location for many years. Some have faced deep disappointments and seen dreams dashed. Through all of this, the sense of community has been profound and blessed.

Across the years, we have seen the value of long-term mentoring relationships, with a focus of Group Listening Prayer, whole-life mentoring, and drawing apart yearly for our retreat.

It has confirmed our conviction that leaders in ministry need safe times, safe places, and safe people to keep going for the long run.

Leading like Jesus
Early in our shaping of the new ministry, a leadership-development specialist asked, "Can you put what you want to accomplish in one

sentence?" I was stumped for a moment. Then these words came, and I spoke them out loud:

"Yes, we want to help young leaders to lead more like Jesus and more to Jesus." Later, I added, "for Jesus."

I had been writing a book on Jesus as a leader and had been reading and rereading Mark's Gospel, noting the marks of Jesus' leadership. Many Christian "leadership" books, it seemed, were largely adapted from secular models—good ones, but not singularly based on Jesus' own leadership, the leadership of a son, a servant, and a shepherd maker.

I decided that we would aim to center on Jesus—through the Word and the Spirit helping young leaders worldwide to lead—to Jesus (in evangelism), like Jesus (in character), and for Jesus (in motive). We began to develop a personalized leadership-development experience, which focused on the character and the competence of ministry leaders, a calling to be Kingdom seekers and not empire builders.

The leadership program was named after the image of an arrow. The image had come to me when I was speaking at Duke Divinity School chapel and was asked how I had seen Billy Graham change across the years. An arrow came to mind. "Billy Graham has been like an arrowhead," I responded, "sharp at the point, as the gospel is always at the forefront in his preaching. He has also grown broader like an arrowhead at its base, as he understands the implications of the gospel for issues like poverty and nuclear weapons, and like the shaft of an arrow in growing deeper in the Lord."

The program continues internationally under other auspices, still aiming to help younger leaders become "sharp arrow[s]" (Isaiah 49:2, NLT) in the Lord's hand—sharp in vision, broad in understanding, and deep in God.

A Mentoring Community
At Arrow sessions, I and others had been teaching about leadership, evangelism, and communication. But increasingly, much of my own

time was spent in long walks and talks with young leaders, listening deeply to their desires and longings, the hopes and hurts of their hearts.

While they were grateful for the teachings, I sensed that most of all they longed for an older leader who would walk with them (without having an agenda to impose) and help them discern what God was saying to them. As we walked together, we were experiencing "holy listening."

Thank you so much for starting our Mentoring Community. These folks in my group have enriched my life immeasurably. Life does not feel so lonely.

DEBORAH, PASTOR AND LEADERSHIP COACH (USA)

Spiritual Mentoring is not quite the same as coaching, counseling, or teaching. All of these are important elements in leadership development and a helpful part of mentoring. The focus of Spiritual Mentoring, however, is to help people pay attention to what God is doing in their lives and respond.

It is not "directing" others in the sense of imposing an agenda on them and telling them what to do. Rather, it is the companionship of a mature friend, who listens deeply, who may ask good questions, and who helps them discern God's calling. Not only do we have the example of Jesus' own mentoring but there is a critical need for leaders in ministry today, with all the pressures they face.

Lon Allison, one of our first Point Groupers, once identified "frenzied busyness" as the highest value of evangelical leaders. The story of his observation is found on pages 40–41. "If that's what we talk most about," he reasons, "it must be what we value most!"

It's a sobering observation. Whether or not it's a "value," I have no doubt that most leaders not only are overly busy but also lead distracted lives in a busy world. Not only are leaders hassled by the external pressures of a busy world and the expectations others place on them but they also live with the internal pressures of dealing with the issues of their own hearts, often by themselves.

I often quote to younger leaders (and to some older ones too) an unusual definition of leadership by the educator Parker Palmer:

> A leader is someone with the power to project either shadow or
> light onto some part of the world and onto the lives of the people
> who dwell there.[4]

They usually respond with a nod and a smile—or a grimace. We can easily think of leaders who are light projectors, and we know others who spread darkness. But within each of us, there are places where light shines and, perhaps unrecognized, shadow places that need to be brought into the light.

In the midst of these pressures, from without and within, where can leaders go for safe places and times of renewal? Where can they find an older (and hopefully wiser and safe) person willing to give them time, listen to their hearts, share their hurts, and help them discern God's agenda for them? That is the question that leads to the need for spiritual companionship and mentoring.

Originals, Not Copies

I am sitting with my young friend Ken in his car outside Tenth Avenue Church in Vancouver, British Columbia, where he has just accepted a call to serve as pastor.

We have known each other now for years, since he was a Wheaton College student who heard me speak and hoped we could meet sometime. We finally connected when he was the student body president at Gordon–Conwell Theological Seminary, and I was a trustee. He offered to drive me to visit some friends, a drive that took several hours. As he drove, I asked him to tell me his story.

I was very impressed, and I put him on my GGTW list and invited him to join our first Arrow cohort, of which he was the youngest. I did watch him—observed his heart for God and others, his keen mind and ability to interact with the training material. As a Japanese Canadian, Ken was somewhat reserved, yet he was well able to relate to the others. In him, I saw both a genuine humility and a clear calling to serve Christ and the gospel.

Ken has often reminded me of the day we sat outside Tenth Church. He had finished seminary and served in a church plant, then felt God call him back to his native Canada, not sure for what or where. As he walked on the beach one day, seeking direction, the words "Tenth Church" came to mind. He was totally surprised. Tenth was a historic old church, once the flagship of its denomination, but it had gone through years of decline. They had had twenty-some pastors in twenty-some years! A remnant of older people were holding on, but it was near to closing.

"I couldn't believe they would want me, in my early thirties, to be their pastor," Ken told me. "But they have called me. And, frankly, I am anxious. I'm not sure I'm up to it."

Ken remembers what I said to him after he poured out his concerns.

"Ken, remember that God is an artist. He doesn't do copies. He does originals. And if you are called here, God will do something new through you."

And that is what God has done. Through the leadership of Ken and others, Tenth Church has made a powerful impact in that very diverse and secular city. The congregation has grown and has become diverse, ethnically and generationally. Worship is fresh. Preaching is strong. New people have come, and as usually happens, a few have left. The church has been recognized with a national award for service to the city. A pimp in the park told a woman in trouble, "Go to Tenth Church. They help people there."

I share Ken's story because I am so thankful for the privilege of helping men and women like him. I could write of many others. I count him, as I do them, not as a "mentoring success" but as a gift from God to his church and the Kingdom. I have watched his growth as a person, as a husband to Sakiko and a father to Joey, as a preacher, an author, and a friend. He often calls me just to see how I am doing. He is truly a son in the Lord, an arrow in a full quiver.

The Friend on the Journey

Jesus was and is the Friend on the journey. "I have called you friends," he told his closest companions at the last, upper-room dinner (John 15:15).

Perhaps the finest biblical portrait of Spiritual Mentoring is that vivid story at the end of Luke's Gospel where two lonely disciples are trudging along, grieved that their Lord is gone. He walks beside them awhile, unrecognized. He listens to their conversation, asks them probing questions, and points them to Scripture explaining that the Messiah had to die. He gently probes their doubts and urges them to believe. Then, accepting their invitation to supper, he sits at the table and breaks and shares the bread. In that moment, they recognize him, and he lights up their lives (Luke 24:13-35). Truly he is the Friend on the journey.

At its best, this is what Spiritual Mentoring is: a long-term companionship together with Christ. It's been said that a spiritual mentor is someone who can remember your own story when you have forgotten it.

> When I joined the Sustain group in the Armidale Diocese, I had never attended a mentoring group like this. It was a deeply encouraging, challenging, and humbling experience. As I'm sure you know, ministry is not always easy, but this group has given me a fresh appreciation for doing life and ministry in fellowship with brothers and sisters who can offer support, encouragement, and advice. I look forward to seeing what God will do in and through our group over the coming years.

My prayer is that many more groups like ours will continue to be formed and meet all over the world so that other brothers and sisters in Christ may be sustained for ministry.

EMMA, PASTOR TRAINEE (AUSTRALIA)

How needy we are, and how blessed, to have such friends.

Acknowledgments

A book is never a solitary journey for its authors. It is resplendent with the care and goodwill of many people. We want to recognize those people who were instrumental in this book adventure.

First and foremost, we are grateful to the Leighton Ford Ministries board, who believed in the importance of this book, particularly to Anne Grizzle, the chair. The board provided funding for a writing retreat and invested in the examination of the book by a writing guide, Dr. Donna K. Wallace. They also secured the input of John Topliff, a former publisher himself and now an agent and spirituality guide. John loved the idea of Mentoring Communities, and he was a great help in the writing process and in securing a publisher for us.

Second, we are indebted to NavPress for taking this book from infancy to maturity with the commitment and sense of companionship that the publisher, Don Pape, gave to us. We are thankful for the editing support of Dave Zimmerman, who was enthusiastic for the value of this book all along the way. We also say thank you to the copyediting brilliance of Elizabeth Schroll, and to Eva Winters and the design team for bringing together our dreams with a cover design.

Finally, this book is the story of mentors and leaders and Mentoring Communities all over the world who tested this concept and created many beautiful expressions of it. This has been a global and Spirit-led adventure where we have journeyed deeply with Christian leaders whom we now call friends. May this book help establish—in strength and faith—the next generation of emerging leaders.

Notes

1: THE URGENT NEED OF EMERGING LEADERS

1. Now known as Chuuk Islands.
2. Susanna Kim, "TLC Documentary on the Resurrection of Former Evangelical Leader," ABC News, January 12, 2011, https://abcnews.go.com/Business/ted -haggard-rebuilds-family-starts-church-leaving-sex/story?id=12566080.
3. Frank Jacobs, "These Are All the World's Major Religions in One Map," World Economic Forum, March 26, 2019, https://www.weforum.org /agenda/2019/03/this-is-the-best-and-simplest-world-map-of-religions/.
4. Margaret Heffernan, "Forget the Pecking Order at Work," TEDWomen, May 2015, https://www.ted.com/talks/margaret_heffernan_why_it_s_time_to _forget_the_pecking_order_at_work. Her talk was based on research in *Genetics and the Behavior of Domestic Animals*, 2nd ed., Temple Grandin and Mark J. Deesing, eds. (London: Academic Press, 2014), 317–59.
5. Heffernan, "Forget the Pecking Order."
6. For a discussion of some issues with a superstar mentality, see Joseph Mattera, "Ten Reasons Some Pastors Develop a Superstar Mentality," *Joseph Mattera* (blog), January 8, 2019, http://josephmattera.org/ten-reasons-pastors -develop-superstar-mentality/.
7. Bill Hybels, *Who You Are When No One's Looking: Choosing Consistency, Resisting Compromise* (Downers Grove, IL: InterVarsity Press, 2014).
8. Kate Shellnutt, "Willow Creek Investigation: Allegations against Bill Hybels Are Credible," *Christianity Today*, February 28, 2019, https://www.christianitytoday .com/news/2019/february/willow-creek-bill-hybels-investigation-iag-report.html.

9. A brief description of the MIT study is found at "True Collaboration: It's Social Capital That Counts," Cofco, accessed October 18, 2019, http://www .cofcogroup.com/true-collaboration-its-social-capital-that-counts/.

10. "Story of Lausanne," Lausanne Movement, accessed October 21, 2019, https://www.lausanne.org/about-the-lausanne-movement.

11. The covenant is available at the Lausanne website: https://www.lausanne.org /content/covenant/lausanne-covenant.

12. Read the Cape Town Commitment at the Lausanne website: https://www .lausanne.org/content/ctc/ctcommitment#capetown.

13. Lausanne Movement, The Cape Town Commitment, accessed October 7, 2019, https://www.lausanne.org/content/ctc/ctcommitment#capetown.

14. Lisa Cannon Green, "Despite Stresses, Few Pastors Give Up on Ministry," LifeWay Research, September 1, 2015, http://lifewayresearch.com /2015/09/01/despite-stresses-few-pastors-give-up-on-ministry/.

15. David Kinnaman, "Burnout & Breakdown: Barna's Risk Metric for Pastors," Barna, January 26, 2017, https://www.barna .com/burnout-breakdown-barnas-risk-metric-pastors/.

16. Lisa Cannon Green, "Former Pastors Report Lack of Support Led to Abandoning Pastorate," LifeWay Research, January 12, 2016, https:// lifewayresearch.com/2016/01/12/former-pastors-report-lack-of-support-led -to-abandoning-pastorate/.

17. Lausanne Movement, "The Cape Town Commitment," 2011, https://www .lausanne.org/content/ctc/ctcommitment#capetown. See section IIE.

18. Leighton Ford, *Transforming Leadership: Jesus' Way of Creating Vision, Shaping Values, and Empowering Change* (Downers Grove, IL: InterVarsity, 1991).

2: WHAT IS SPIRITUAL MENTORING?

1. J. John, email message to author and Leighton Ford, July 18, 2017.

2. I first heard him say this at a plenary presentation in Eldoret, Kenya, on July 8, 2015.

3. See, for example, Robby Gallaty, *Rediscovering Discipleship: Making Jesus' Final Words Our First Work* (Grand Rapids, MI: Zondervan, 2015), chap. 9.

4. Kibeom Lee and Michael C. Ashton, *The H Factor of Personality: Why Some People are Manipulative, Self-Entitled, Materialistic, and Exploitive—and Why It Matters for Everyone* (Waterloo, Ontario: Wilfrid Laurier University Press, 2012), 17.

5. Lausanne Movement, "The Cape Town Commitment," 2011, https://www .lausanne.org/content/ctc/ctcommitment.

6. I last heard Mark say this during a presentation on mentoring evangelists at the Bellfry in Lexington, Virginia, on May 23, 2018.

7. I last heard Raphaël say this during a presentation on Mentoring Communities given in Karen, Kenya, on April 4, 2016.

8. Leighton Ford Ministries, "Billy Graham on What He Would Do if He Were Starting Ministry Again," February 6, 2015, https://www.leightonfordministries .org/2015/02/06/billy-graham-on-what-he-would-do-if-he-were-starting -ministry-again/.

NOTES

3: SAFE TIMES, SAFE PLACES, SAFE PEOPLE
1. Shared by Lon Allison at our initial Rock Hill Gathering in South Carolina, March 29, 2006.
2. See Matthew 25:21.

4: MENTORING COMMUNITIES IN THE BIBLE
1. David Ruiz, as quoted in "The Lausanne Covenant," Lausanne Movement, accessed November 5, 2019, https://www.lausanne.org/content/covenant/lausanne-covenant.
2. Lausanne Movement, The Cape Town Commitment, accessed October 7, 2019, https://www.lausanne.org/content/ctc/ctcommitment#capetown.

5: SOLITUDE
1. As quoted in Constance FitzGerald, "From Impasse to Prophetic Hope: Crisis of Memory," in *Carmelite Wisdom and Prophetic Hope: Treasures Both New and Old*, Mary Frohlich, ed. (Washington, DC: ICS Publications, 2018), 179–180.
2. From "The Sayings of Light and Love," in *The Collected Works of St. John of the Cross*, third ed. (Washington, DC: ICS Publications, 2017), 95.
3. From Book One in *The Collected Works of St. John of the Cross*, third ed. (Washington, DC: ICS Publications, 2017), chap. 5.
4. As quoted in Richard H. Bell and Barbara L. Battin, eds., *Seeds of the Spirit: Wisdom of the Twentieth Century* (Louisville, KY: Westminster John Knox Press, 1995), 104.
5. Gunilla Norris, *Sharing Silence* (Bell Tower, 1993), 31.

6: PRAYER AND BIBLE REFLECTION
1. Eugene H. Peterson, *Christ Plays in Ten Thousand Places: A Conversation in Spiritual Theology* (Grand Rapids, MI: Eerdmans, 2005), 107–108. Emphasis added.
2. Amos Yong, *The Bible, Disability, and the Church: A New Vision of the People of God* (Grand Rapids, MI: Eerdmans, 2011).
3. Richard Foster, *Prayer: Finding the Heart's True Home* (New York: HarperSanFrancisco, 1992), 13.
4. Dennis Linn, Sheila Fabricant Linn, and Matthew Linn, *Sleeping with Bread: Holding What Gives You Life* (Mahwah, NJ: Paulist, 1995), 3.
5. Celtic Daily Prayer: Prayers and Readings from the Northumbria Community (New York: HarperCollins, 2002), 25. Language was updated for modern readers.

7: LISTENING
1. Peter F. Drucker, *The Daily Drucker: 366 Days of Insight and Motivation for Getting the Right Things Done* (New York: Routledge, 2011), April 11.
2. Warren Bennis and Burt Nanus, *Leaders: Strategies for Taking Charge*, 2nd ed. (New York: HarperBusiness, 2003), 89.
3. Aelred of Rievaulx, *Spiritual Friendship*, Lawrence C. Braceland, trans. (Collegeville, MN: Liturgical Press, 2010), 55.

4. Henri J. M. Nouwen, *Making All Things New: An Invitation to the Spiritual Life* (New York: HarperSanFrancisco, 2002), 50.
5. Henri J. M. Nouwen, *You Are the Beloved: Daily Meditations for Spiritual Living* (New York: Convergent, 2017), 152.
6. Keith Miller, *The Taste of New Wine: A Book about Life* (Austin, TX: Formation Press, 2009), 89.
7. "Hear him, ye deaf" from Charles Wesley (lyrics), "O for a Thousand Tongues to Sing," 1739, public domain.
8. As quoted in Madeleine L'Engle, *Walking on Water: Reflections on Faith and Art* (New York: Convergent, 2016), 8.
9. L'Engle, *Walking on Water*, 13, 15.
10. Wendell Berry, *A Timbered Choir: The Sabbath Poems 1979–1997* (Washington, DC: Counterpoint, 1998), 207.
11. To view an image of this painting, see http://www.benlongfineart.com /first-presbyterian-church.
12. Rachel Naomi Remen, *Kitchen Table Wisdom: Stories That Heal* (New York: Penguin Books, 2006), 220.
13. Quoted in L'Engle, *Walking on Water*, 21.
14. Alan Jones, *Passion for Pilgrimage: Notes for the Journey Home* (New York: Morehouse, 1999), 70.
15. Kenneth Paul Kramer, *Redeeming Time: T. S. Eliot's* Four Quartets (Lanham, MD: Cowley, 2007), 87.
16. Berry, *A Timbered Choir*, 147.
17. Gerard Manley Hopkins, from "As Kingfishers Catch Fire" in *Mortal Beauty, God's Grace: Major Poems and Spiritual Writings of Gerard Manley Hopkins* (New York: Vintage Books, 2003), 23.
18. Lloyd John Ogilvie, *You Are Loved and Forgiven: Paul's Letter of Hope to the Colossians* (Glendale, CA: G/L Publications, 1977), 57.

8: QUESTIONS

1. This chapter is an adaptation of my article "The Art of Asking Spiritual Questions: 'Noticing the Duck,'" *Presence* 15, no. 1 (September 2009), 51–58, available here: https://digitalcommons.georgefox.edu/cgi/viewcontent .cgi?article=1021&context=gfes.
2. The focus of spiritual companionship is a person's relationship to God. The focus of counseling or therapy is a person's relationship to herself or himself and to others. The focus of discipling is a person's relationship to God in the context of a faith's theology and spiritual traditions.
3. Ignatius lived between 1491 and 1556. He is known for his *Spiritual Exercises*, a book of prayers, devotions, and exercises carried out over thirty days. Many people today use *Spiritual Exercises* to deepen their faith.
4. Rainer Maria Rilke, *Letters to a Young Poet* (New York: W. W. Norton, 1993), 27.

9: DISCERNMENT

1. Leighton Ford is quoted in this chapter from his unpublished 2013 article "The Gift of Listening: The Call of the LFM Mentoring Community," which is

available here: https://www.leightonfordministries.org/wp-content
/uploads/2019/04/The-Gift-of-Listening-by-Leighton-Ford-1.pdf.

2. To read about this, see Timothy Mackie, "What Is the Shema?" *The Bible Project* (blog), February 18, 2017, https://thebibleproject.com/blog/what-is-the-shema/.

3. Leighton Ford, *The Attentive Life: Discerning God's Presence in All Things* (Downers Grove, IL: InterVarsity, 2008).

10: GROUP LISTENING PRAYER

1. Psalm 5:3; 27:14; 38:15; 40:1-2; 130.

2. Rose Mary Dougherty, *Group Spiritual Direction: Community for Discernment* (New York: Paulist Press, 1995).

3. Rose Mary Doughterty, *Group Spiritual Direction*, 14.

12: BUILDING AND SUSTAINING A MENTORING COMMUNITY

1. Material for this extract and the previous two paragraphs was heavily inspired by that found here: https://www.leightonfordministries.org/leadership/.

2. Kathleen Norris, *Acedia and me: A Marriage, Monks, and a Writer's Life* (New York: Riverhead Books, 2008), 34, xix.

AFTERWORD

1. Billy Graham passed away February 21, 2018, from natural causes, at the age of ninety-nine.

2. "Religion: A Challenge from Evangelicals," *Time*, August 5, 1974.

3. Lauren F. Winner, "From Mass Evangelist to Soul Friend," *Christianity Today*, October 2, 2000, https://www.christianitytoday.com/ct/2000/october2/7.56 .html.

4. Parker J. Palmer, *Let Your Life Speak: Listening for the Voice of Vocation* (San Francisco: Jossey-Bass, 2000), 78.

CONNECT · DISCOVER · TRANSFORM

Lifelong Leadership is the culmination of a long conversation shepherded by Leighton Ford, honorary lifetime chair of the Lausanne Movement, who since 1985 has worked to identify and mentor emerging ministry leaders.

Leighton Ford Ministries is a catalyst for **mentoring** a new generation of **healthy leaders** who sustain **thriving ministries** for the sake of the gospel. In partnership with Dr. MaryKate Morse and other leaders, LFM sponsors and supports Mentoring Communities for ministry leaders around the world and serves as a catalyst for churches and parachurch organizations launching mentoring ministries of their own.

WWW.LFMCONNECT.ORG
FACEBOOK.COM/LFMCONNECT
TWITTER.COM/@LEIGHTONFORDMIN

The Lausanne Movement also connects younger leaders with mentors in pursuit of mission, character, and friendship.
Learn more at **LAUSANNE.ORG/YLGEN**

CP1603